FRANK LLOYD WRIGHT
SELECTED HOUSES
3

*Copyright © 1989 A.D.A. EDITA Tokyo Co., Ltd.*
*3-12-14 Sendagaya, Shibuya-ku, Tokyo 151, Japan*
*All rights reserved. No part of this publication may be reproduced,*
*stored in a retrieval system, or transmitted, in any form or by any means,*
*electronic, mechanical, photocopying, recording, or otherwise,*
*without permission in writing from the publisher.*

*The drawings of Frank Lloyd Wright are*
*Copyright © The Frank Lloyd Wright Foundation 1989*
*Text Copyright © The Frank Lloyd Wright Foundation 1989*
*Copyright of Photographs © 1989 RETORIA: Y. Futagawa & Associated Photographers*

*The red square with FRANK LLOYD WRIGHT in block letters is a*
*registered trademark belonging to The Frank Lloyd Wright Foundation.*
*The Frank Lloyd Wright Foundation grants permission for*
*A.D.A. EDITA Tokyo to use the mark in its block.*

*Design: Gan Hosoya*

*First published 1989*
*Reprinted, 1992*

*ISBN 4-87140-545-1 C1352*

*Printed and bound in Japan*

# FRANK LLOYD WRIGHT SELECTED HOUSES 3

## TALIESIN WEST

TEXT BY BRUCE BROOKS PFEIFFER
EDITED AND PHOTOGRAPHED BY YUKIO FUTAGAWA

A.D.A. EDITA Tokyo

# Taliesin West: Bruce Brooks Pfeiffer
文：ブルース・ブルックス・ファイファー

At the age of seventy, a time when most men have already long retired from active life, Frank Lloyd Wright, accompanied by his wife and about thirty young men and women who were his apprentices in architecture, came upon a vast, unpopulated sweep of land on the Arizona desert at the foot of the McDowell Mountains. They placed sleeping bags and rudimentary camping equipment on the desert floor, and began their life of clearing the ground, building temporary shelters, and preparing the site for the erection of a new building. This new building was to be a southwestern headquarters — living quarters, studio, home and workshop for the Taliesin Fellowship. Established in 1932, the Taliesin Fellowship was an apprenticeship training experiment in the lines of architectural education. It was barely 5 years old when Mr. and Mrs. Wright decided that living in Wisconsin during the winter months was cramping the style of the group of people who were learning not only by following and participating in the work of a great master, but were also learning the art and craft of architecture by actually constructing buildings. Wisconsin winters were notoriously cold; just about all the energy one had was spent in keeping warm: felling trees and cutting firewood for the many fireplaces at Taliesin that were burning continually from the end of October to early March or April. Now, in this winter of 1937-38, they had left their Wisconsin home Taliesin behind in blizzards and subzero weather and migrated across the great American prairies to the warm southwest land of Arizona and there began the building of Taliesin West. This was not the first contact with the Arizona desert for the Wrights.

In 1927 Frank Lloyd Wright had first come there with his wife Olgivanna and their two daughters Svetlana and Iovanna to take part in the design and building of the Arizona Biltmore Hotel, a new resort for Phoenix. During the years 1927 and 1928 the Wrights, living in a rented house in Phoenix, experienced the dry, clear air of the southwest, from early winter into hot spring and summer. Phoenix, albeit the capitol of Arizona, was hardly more than a "cow-town," where much business connected with cattle ranching was conducted. The atmosphere of the town was new, raw and relaxed, and permeated with a friendliness often evident in pioneering cities. Everyone, except the native Indians and Hispanics, was an "immigrant" who had come to this land on the Sonoran desert to find and create a new life, with new opportunities.

While working on the Biltmore Mr. Wright met Dr. Alexander Chandler, of the town that took his name, some miles south of Phoenix. Before the Phoenix and neighboring Scottsdale regions became tourist areas, Chandler, with its Spanish-style San Marcos Hotel, had been the tourist center of this part of the southwest.

多くの人が第一線を退いてすでに久しい70歳という年齢で、ライトは妻と34人の弟子たちを引き連れてマクダウェル山系の麓、アリゾナ砂漠の人里離れた地にやって来た。寝袋と若干のキャンプ用具の荷を解くや、敷地の清掃、現場小屋作り、整地などに忙しい生活にとりかかった。新しい建物はタリアセン・フェローシップの南西部の拠点として、生活の場とスタジオ、それに宿泊施設と作業場を兼ねたものになるはずだった。1932年に設立されたタリアセン・フェローシップは徒弟制の訓練によって建築教育を行なうという実験的な試みを続けていた。巨匠の傍らにあってその仕事に携わり、現実に建物を建てる作業にも加わることで建築の技術を学ぼうという人々にウィスコンシンの厳寒の中で過ごさせるのはいささか過酷だと、ライト夫妻が決心を固めたのは、その5年前のことだった。ウィスコンシンの冬の寒さのほどは並大抵のものではなく、人間の持ち合わせているエネルギーのことごとくが身体を暖めることに使い果たされてしまう。木を伐り倒し薪をつくってはタリアセンのあちらこちらにある暖炉にくべて、10月の終わりから3月か4月の初めまで火を絶やせない。とうとう1937年から38年にかけての冬、寒風吹きすさぶ氷点下の、ウィスコンシンのタリアセンをあとにして、アメリカの大草原を越えて南西の地アリゾナへ移り、タリアセン・ウェストの建設にとりかかった。けれども、ライトたちにとってはこれがアリゾナの砂漠との初めてのかかわりではなかった。

1927年、ライトは妻オルジヴァンナのほかにスヴェトラーナとイオヴァンナの二人の娘を伴ってはじめてアリゾナを訪れていた。フェニックスの新しいリゾートであるアリゾナ・ビルトモア・ホテルを設計するためであった。この年から1928年にかけて、ライト一家はフェニックスに家を借りて生活し、初冬から春、さらに夏の暑さまでを過ごしたから、その乾燥し、澄み切った空気を身をもって知っていた。アリゾナの首都でありながらフェニックスは「牛の町」を脱し切れず、産業の多くのものが牧畜と何らかの形で結びついている状態だったが、それだけ町は若々しく素朴でくつろいだ雰囲気に満ち、開拓者の町によくある仲間意識の強い所だった。先住民であるインディアンやラテン・アメリカ系の人々のほかはだれもが「移住者」で、ソノラン砂漠にあるこの地に、好運の待ちうける新しい生活を見つけ、あるいは作り出そうとやって来た人々であった。

ライトがアレクサンダー・チャンドラー博士に会ったのは、フェニックスの南数マイルの彼の名を冠した町にビルトモア・ホテルの設計を進める時だった。フェニックスと、それに隣接するスコッツデールの一帯が観光地になる以前から、スパニッシュ・スタイルのサン・マルコス・ホテルの持主だったチャンドラー博士は、元は中西部からアリゾナへやって来た獣医だった。このあたりで採れる綿がゴムタイヤの材料に最適であることを発見した彼は、すぐに開拓と綿花の栽培にとりかかり、やがて財をなしそれ

Dr. Chandler, a veterinarian from the Midwest who came to Arizona, discovered that cotton grown in this region was ideal for the manufacture of rubber tires. He soon went into land development and cotton growing, and quickly built up a fortune which he turned into the tourist business. He dreamed of a new hotel resort, and asked Frank Lloyd Wright to be his architect. The resort was to be called San Marcos-in-the-Desert, so as to differentiate it from the existing Hotel San Marcos, and it would be located out on the desert on the southern slopes of South Mountain. The following season Mr. Wright, again with his wife and two daughters, but this time with a staff of architectural draftsmen, came once again south out of the Wisconsin blizzards to live in Chandler and go to work on the great hotel scheme.

For living quarters, this time of 1928-1929, he elected not to rent space in town, but to move out onto the desert and build something for his family and his architectural office. The result of that choice was the famous desert camp "Ocotilla."

The Ocotilla camp is an important element in the history of Taliesin West because of its use of textiles for an overhead roofing. While he was working on his Autobiography, he was also building Ocotilla, and his own description of the camp has the sense of something in the making rather than the description of a finished building.

"The box-board cabins," he wrote, "are connected by a low box-board wall with a horizontal zigzag — for the same reason Thomas Jefferson worm-walled his brick." [The reference is to the low brick serpentine wall Jefferson designed for his buildings at the University of Virginia. ed.] "It will be self-supporting and this will complete the compound. Necessary openings on the canvas-topped box buildings we will close with canvas-covered wood frames. Flaps hinged with rubber belting. No glazed doors or windows. Glass is not for this type of desert camp if indeed glass belongs in the desert at all.

"Now, when all these white canvas wings, like sails, are spread, the buildings will look something like ships coming down the mesa, rigged like ships balanced in the breeze.

"Yes, the group will look like some new kind of desert fleet. We painted the horizontal boards with cold-water paint, continuing around the varied board wall connecting all the cabins about the mound. I chose dry-rose as the color to match the light on the desert floor. The one-two triangle we used in planning the camp is made by the mountain ranges about the site. And the one-two triangle is the cross section of the talus at their bases. This triangle is reflected in the general

を観光事業に投じたのである。彼は新たにホテルを中心としたリゾートを心に描き，ライトを建築家として選んだのであった。このリゾートは，もとのホテル・サン・マルコスと区別するために「サン・マルコス・イン・ザ・デザート」と呼ばれ，サウス・マウンテンの南斜面の砂漠のはずれに建てられる予定だった。次のシーズンにもライトは妻子を伴って来たが，今度はドラフトマンのスタッフも同行して，ウィスコンシンの風雪をあとに再にやって来ると，ホテルの大設計をまとめるべくチャンドラーに居を定めた。

1928年から1929年にかけてのこの時は，町で部屋を借りずに，砂漠の只中に乗りこんで家族の生活と設計の場とした。この選択の結果が，のちに名高い砂漠のキャンプ「オコティラ」を生んだ。

オコティラ・キャンプがタリアセンの歴史の中でも重要な位置を占めているのは，屋根に布を使ったという点にある。ライトが自伝を執筆していた時期は，オコティラをつくっている時と一致しているのだが，文中のこのキャンプについての語り方を見るとここを完成された建物というよりは，つねに建設中のものとして考えていたようだ。

「ボックス・ボード・キャビンは」と彼自身書いている。「トマス・ジェファーソンが煉瓦の壁でそうしたのと同じ理由で，凹凸の多い平面を持つ低いボックス・ボードの壁でつながれている。」（これはジェファーソンがヴァージニア大学の彼の建物を設計した時の煉瓦造の低い壁のことである。）「この壁は構造的には自立しながら，複合体を一体化する要素であった。キャンヴァスの屋根をつけた箱型の建物に必要に応じて設けられた開口部には木製の枠にキャンヴァス張りの蓋をつける。丁番にはゴムの帯を取り付けた。ドアにも窓にもガラスは使わない。仮に砂漠でガラスを使うことがあるとしても，このようなタイプの，砂漠のキャンプにだけはガラスは向いていない。」

「この白いキャンヴァスの建物が完成して，あたりに広がれば，さながら帆に風をはらんだ船が台地の海を滑って来るように見えるだろう。」

「まるで，砂漠の船団ではないか。種々の板張りの壁のまわりを包むように，丘に散らばるキャビンをつないで水平に伸びる板を水性のペンキで塗装した。砂漠の光に似合う色としてドライ・ローズを私は選んだ。このキャンプのデザインに使った2:1の勾配の三角形のパターンは，敷地のまわりの山に合わせたものだ。2:1の三角形は基礎まわりの断面と同じなのである。この三角形は，平面形をはじめ，キャビンの形態のいたるところに使われている。妻面のキャンヴァスを真紅に塗った赤い三角形が，ほかでもない私たちがこのキャンプをオカティロ（原文のママ）と呼ぶ理由なのだ。ろうそくの炎を意味する言葉なのである。」

「白い光を放つ頭上のキャンヴァスと窓代わりのキャンヴァスが，かくも心地良い光を室内にゆきわ

forms of all the cabins as well as the general plan. We will paint the canvas triangles in the eccentric gables, scarlet. The red triangular form in the treatment is why we call the camp Ocatillo *(sic)*. Candle flame.

"I presently found that the white luminous canvas overhead and canvas used instead of windows afforded such agreeable diffusion of light within, was so enjoyable and sympathetic to the desert, that I now felt more oppressed by the thought of the opaque solid overhead of the much too heavy Midwestern house.

"The desert devils would come whirling like a dancing dervish and go in drifting spirals of dust high in the air. Occasionally a devil would cross the camp and it would shudder in its grasp like a ship — but hold fast. No damage.

"I believe we pay too slight attention to making slight buildings beautiful or beautiful buildings slight. Lightness and strength may now be synonymous.

"Usually we spend so much too much to make buildings last, as we say. Unqualified to build, we are still busy making caves for survival.

"So, Ocatillo — our little desert camp — you are an ephemera.

"The little camp is finished. We love it. The canvas windows of Ocatillo are like ship sails when open and may shut against dust or may open part way to deflect desert breezes into the interiors. Screened openings for cross ventilation are everywhere at the floor levels, a discovery I made in seeking coolness, to be used during the heat of the day; closed at night. The long sides of the canvas slopes lie easily with the lines of the landscape stretching themselves wide open toward the sun in order to aid a little in warming the interiors in winter. This long canvas roof-side is to have additional cover of canvas, air blowing between the two sheets, if the camp is ever occupied in the summer. We can add this later if we stay on in summer, and make it belong.

"Finally to justify our wild adventure, Ocatillo cost not so much more than the rent and keep asked for equivalent accommodations in Chandler or in Phoenix for the one season we were to stay. The cost was about two hundred dollars per cabin. The labor was mostly our own. We are the better for that labor. We have met the desert, loved it and lived with it, and the desert is ours."

The final engineering and working drawings for San Marcos-in-the-Desert were completed that first season living and working at Ocotilla. But as the spring and pending summer's heat came on, they were forced to move out and go north to Wisconsin. They planned to return in the autumn, when construction for the hotel resort was scheduled, and resume work in Ocotilla supervising the building of San Marcos. The hotel site was located not far from the little desert camp, over the

たらせると，それが楽しく砂漠にふさわしいので中西部の重々しすぎる住宅の，くすんだ堅い屋根が頭上を蔽ううっとうしさをこれまでになく感じさせられるのだった。」

「砂漠の悪魔は，さながら踊る托鉢僧のように旋回しながらやって来ては，空高く埃を舞い上げていずこへともなく去ってゆく。時にはこの悪魔がやって来て，海の船のようにキャンプをもてあそぼうとした。けれども，その時には船の帆よろしくキャンヴァスをしっかりとたためば何の被害もなく去ってゆく。」

「これまで，軽い建築を美しく，あるいは美しい建築を軽くしようとすることが，余りに少なかった。軽さと強さは今や同義語になったのだ。」

「つねに私たちは建物を長持ちさせることに労力と費用を注ぎ過ぎた。いまもって，建築を作ろうとして，せっせと洞窟を作っているようなものだ。」

「それにひきかえオカティロ――私たちの小さな砂漠のキャンプよ――おまえは，蜻蛉のようなもの。」

「小さなキャンプはできあがった。私たちはこれを愛している。オカティロの，キャンヴァスを張った窓は，開けば船の帆のようだが，埃をよけるためには閉じることもできるし，一部を開けば砂漠の風を家の中に迎えることもできる。風通しのための，網戸をつけた開口は床の高さのいたるところに設けられている。日中の暑さになんとかして涼しさを取り入れようと考え出したものだが，夜には閉じられる。キャンヴァスの屋根の広い方の斜面は周囲の景色に合わせるようにおだやかに広がり，冬の室内を暖める一助ともなっている。この屋根面にキャンヴァスのカバーを重ねれば，夏には2枚のキャンヴァスの間を風が通り抜け，屋根の温度を下げる。」

「さらに，自然の中での私たちの冒険について付け加えておきたいことがある。チャンドラーやフェニックスで同程度の広さや設備を備えた所をひと冬借りればその家賃や維持費はオカティロの建築費用と，さして違いがない。工事費はキャビンひとつあたり，およそ200ドルで，労働力は大部分を自前で賄った。我々も，労働力としてあながち捨てたものではない。私たちは砂漠と出逢い，砂漠を愛し，生活を共にした。いまや砂漠は我々のものになっているのだ。」

サン・マルコス・イン・ザ・デザートの最終実施図は，初めてのシーズンをオコティラで生活し働きながら完成された。けれども，春と，それに続いて夏の暑さが来ると，さすがに北のウィスコンシンへ移動せざるをえなくなった。予定ではホテルの建設が始まればオコティラでの仕事を再開してサン・マルコスの建築の監理にあたるはずだった。ホテルの敷地は，砂漠の小さなキャンプからほど遠からぬ，隣の丘を越えた谷にあったのである。

ところが1929年10月の株の大暴落が，建築の望みを霧消させた。このプロジェクトの作業は中止

adjacent hill in the next valley.

But the stock market collapse in October of 1929 dissolved any hopes of building. Work on the project was brought to a halt, and the Wrights did not return to Arizona. Ocotilla did not last but the one season; a fire consumed part of it, and the local neighbors, when the camp was deserted, took away the rest. Truly an ephemera, as the architect described it, Ocotilla is recorded only by photography; the little desert camp so cherished by the Wrights and their draftsmen is gone forever, but it was one of the most charming examples of architecture in and for the desert that ever existed.

Many of the lessons learned in its construction, and experienced while living in it, came to fruition ten years later in his design for this new desert camp up on the desert below the McDowell Mountains. Taliesin West was also planned as a canvas-topped structure. But in place of the perishable wood supports used in Ocotilla, the abundance of native stone, richly varied in color and shapes scattered across the desert floor at the foot of the hills, made possible a supporting structure of concrete and stone masonry.

The site and its relation to the mountain range to the north dictated the orientation of the plan. The axis is derived from this extended view, from the west, looking east to a group of isolated mountains: Black Mountain and Granite Reef Mountain. No building, if Mr. Wright could help it, was ever placed on a direct northing-south axis. If it were, he explained to us, the building would have a permanently hot side (south) and a cold side (north). By tilting the plan off the direct compass points the sun and shade had their play throughout all the rooms and vistas throughout the year. Taliesin West was planned with the same object in mind. The prow, an extended terrace with sunken garden, points south by southwest, looking over Paradise Valley and to the Camelback Mountains in Scottsdale at the other side of the valley. The term "prow," used by the architect from the very inception of the plan, once again brings the simile of a ship on the desert into focus, as it was with the little cabins of Ocotilla — "like a fleet of little ships."

Unlike its predecessor Ocotilla, Taliesin West was not planned as a group of buildings or little cabins, but as one opus set on concrete terraces, surrounded by massive low masonry walls. The very first sketches for the work were those that designated how the earth was to be moved and relocated to accommodate the design of the whole building in relation to the site. Blocked-off areas, in different colors, made clear how the terraces were to conform to the topography without taking away or bringing in any additional soil for fill or excavation. The total plan

され，ライトはもうアリゾナに戻らなかった。オコティラは，ひと冬で使命を終えたのである。火事でその一部を失い，土地の住民たちは，キャンプが使われなくなると資材を持ち去った。ライトがそう表現した通りに，まさしく蜻蛉のような生を生きたオコティラは，わずかに写真にあとを留めるばかりである。ライトとドラフトマンたちにたいそう大切にされた，砂漠の小キャンプは，永遠に甦ることはなかったが，砂漠に作られた砂漠のための建築の中でもこれは最も魅力的なもののひとつであった。

これを建設する中で学んだ多くのもの，ここでの生活の多くの体験は，マクダウェル山系の麓の砂漠につくられる新しいキャンプの設計に，10年の時を隔てて結実することになった。タリアセン・ウェストもやはりキャンヴァスの屋根を持つ建築として計画された。だが，オコティラで使われた傷みやすい木材に代わるものとして丘陵の麓の砂漠のいたるところに色も形も様々な自然石が豊富にあったので，これを利用してコンクリートと石積の構造体が可能になった。

敷地と，その北に位置する山脈との関係で決定された建物の方向は，東から西へと続くブラック・マウンテンとグラナイト・リーフ・マウンテンの山々を望む雄大な景観に向くよう軸が定められた。ライトは建物を真南と北に向けて建てることはなかった。そんなことをすれば，建物の一面（南）は年中暑い半面，裏（北）はいつも寒い日陰になってしまうというのだ。平面を磁石の針の向きからわずかに振ることで，どの部屋にも，また，どの景色にも日向と日陰が交互に現われるという訳である。タリアセン・ウェストでもこの考え方は変わらなかった。サンクン・ガーデンに続く，突き出したテラスは南から南西にかけての方向を向いて，パラダイス・ヴァレーをはさんで向こう側のスコッツデールのキャメルバック・マウンテンを望む。「舳先」ということばが，計画の当初からライトによって使われ，オコティラの小さなキャビンの集合が「小船の船団を思わせる」と表現されたのと同じように，砂漠に浮かぶ船という比喩がここでも再び使われた。

かつてのオコティラが群としての建築，あるいはキャビンの集合という形であったのに対してタリアセン・ウェストは，コンクリートのテラスの上に載る低い石積の壁に囲われた一体の建築として計画された。この作品の最初に描かれたスケッチは，敷地と建物全体の関わり方を検討するための，土工事のものだった。そこでは，地形に合わせてテラスを作り，根伐りや盛土によって敷地外と土のやりとりが生じないよう種々の色を使って，それぞれの部分を囲んで検討されていた。全体計画は設計のごく初期の段階で決められた。この，初期のスケッチを思い起こして，ライトは私たちに言ったものだ。砂漠は彼にとって天の啓示のようなものだったと。「私は砂漠の美しさにうたれた。強烈な太陽にさらされて乾き，澄み切った空気，峻厳な山々の地形，そうした砂漠地帯というものの全体が，私の生まれ育っ

was set very early in the design stages. Frank Lloyd Wright, in remembering his work on these first sketches, told us that the desert was like a revelation to him. ". . . I was struck by the beauty of the desert, by the dry, clear sun-drenched air, by the stark geometry of the mountains, the entire region was an inspiration in strong contrast to the lush, pastoral landscape of my native Wisconsin. And out of that experience, a revelation is what I guess you might call it, came the design for these buildings. The design sprang out of itself, with no precedent and nothing following it. The wish to use white canvas for toplight came, of course, as a result of the season we spent living in Ocotilla. I found that light to be so desirable that I was determined to explore it further in these buildings. But here the use of masonry, redwood and canvas combined is new in every aspect."

Since Taliesin West was to be the winter headquarters for an architect's studio and workshop, the first structure that was built was the stone "vault" at the far end of the large Drafting Room — a safe-keeping place for the drawings. At the other end, a tall square mass housed the kitchen and serving area, the Drafting Room adjacent. No partitions separated Drafting Room from kitchen. Until further structures were added the Drafting Room served for dining, social gathering, and musical concerts, as well as architectural drawing. Also no partitions separated the long Drafting Room from the walkway — the Pergola — on its north side. While using the room for dining, thus open to the elements, the wind and the cold, Mrs. Wright recollected that "On cold mornings, even with a great fire in the fireplace, we had to eat with mittens on because the silverware was so icy cold!"

The only totally closed-in area was the stone vault at the far west end of the Drafting Room. It was in this structure, the stone vault, that the grammar of the whole — the desert masonry — was first executed. Up to this time — the winter of 1937-38, there had been no masonry on record that resembled this particular solution. And as is always the case, it was in the problem that Mr. Wright found the solution. The problem was how to build with native stone that could not be tailored or cut, like limestone, granite, sandstone or marble; how to build a strong masonry wall with minimum expense and minimum use of skilled labor. Since most of the available stones had a smooth, flat face on one side, the solution presented itself thus: place the smooth surface into a temporary wooden form, the curved boulder-like part of the stone remaining in the center of the wall like "fill," pour concrete around the stone, moving up the surface of the wall inside the form with more stones, and more rubble-fill as required. Once set, in a day or so in this dry atmosphere, the form could be stripped, taken apart, and the lumber used over

たウィスコンシンの，のどかで緑ゆたかな田園風景とは際立った対比を示していた。このような，啓示とも呼ぶべき体験からこの建物の設計が生まれた。設計とはおのずから生まれるものであって，何らかの先例によって生まれるものでもなく，それを先例として何かが追従するべきものでもない。白いキャンヴァスをトップライトに使いたいと思ったのは，もちろん，我々がオコティラで過ごした経験によるものだ。そこで，光はたいそう重要なものだと身をもって知ったからこそこの建築では，さらに踏みこんで光と正面から取り組もうと思ったにすぎないのだが，ここでの，石積とレッドウッドとキャンヴァスの組み合わせ方は，どの面からとりあげても新しいものとなった。」

タリアセン・ウェストはライトの冬だけのスタジオ兼作業場にするつもりだったから，初めに建てられた建物は，製図室のはずれに位置する図面の保管所，石の「ヴォールト」であった。製図室を挟んでその反対側の高い正方形のマッスの中には厨房とサーヴィス・エリアがあった。製図室と厨房の間には間仕切がない。のちに増築されるまで，製図室は図面を描くばかりではなく食堂にも，集会にもコンサートにも使われていた。細長い製図室とその北側の，パーゴラと呼ばれた通路との間にも仕切はなかった。ここでの，風と寒さにさらされる食事を思い出しながらライト夫人は当時を振り返ってはこう言ったものだ。「寒い朝には暖炉の火がどんなに煌々と燃えていようと手袋をして食事をしなければならなかった。銀の食器がまるで氷みたいに冷たかったからね」と。

ただひとつ完全に閉じることのできたのは製図室の西のはずれにある石のヴォールトであった。この時，すなわち1937年から38年にかけての冬までに，ここで試みられた独創的な方法に類する石積の記録はない。いつものように，ライトのこの解決法は問題そのものの中から生み出されたものだった。問題とは，ふつうの石灰岩，花崗岩，砂岩や大理石のようなきちんと加工された石ではなく自然の石をそのまま使ってどう積めばいいかということだった。最小の費用と最小限の熟練した労働力でどう作るかである。大部分の石が一面のみ平らだったので次のような工法が考え出された。石の平らな面を仮枠に向けておき，玉石状の部分を壁の内側に向け，骨材のようにして，そこにコンクリートを流し込む。コンクリートが序々に上って来るにしたがって石と割栗を必要に応じて加えてゆくのである。コンクリートを打ち終わると，乾燥した空気の中では1日ないし2日で仮枠を外すことができ，仮枠を繰返し使用しながら壁作りは続けられる。壁の独特のモザイク状の模様はこうした石の色と形によるものなのである。この重量感のある構造壁の美しさは，それ自体が芸術であることを意識しつつ注意深く石を選び，積んでいったからにほかならなかった。表面が平らでない石を積んでしまったときのこと，コンクリートがこの石の表面に流れ込んで表面を蔽ってしまうのを気づかうライトの指示によって，「あひるの卵」と私たち

again to continue the wall or walls as desired. It was from the variety of the colors and shapes that the wall took its character, truly mosaic-like, as a whole. Throughout all of this heavy construction, it was the artistic and carefully chosen placement of the stones that determined the resultant beauty of the wall as a whole. When a particular stone's surface was not absolutely flat, with the possibility of the concrete running down onto the face of the stone, Mr. Wright directed us to place round river stones, called "goose-eggs" along the upper part of the face stone to prevent the seepage of the wet concrete onto the surface. Again, in this solution came a startling result of jagged angular large face stones lined with an edge of these small smooth rocks, usually lavender and grey in color. The contrast of the two produces a kind of melodic and rhythmic play across the walls of the buildings.

On an outing the Fellowship made to northern Arizona into one of the canyons which had once been under water, the deep, horizontal grooves in the stone canyon walls caused by water erosion greatly appealed to Mr. Wright. On his return to camp he instructed the apprentices building the walls to insert triangular strips of wood stretching in thin lines on the inside surface of the wooden forms prior to placing stones and pouring concrete. When the forms were removed the indentation of the horizontal strips left an impression within the concrete surface of the wall, creating yet another element with which the sun could make deep shadow lines across the mosaic wall. This element of the sun and shadow was, from the beginning of construction, an important design consideration throughout Taliesin West.

"The desert abhors the straight, hard line," he told us. And he sited, as examples, the desert flora — the cactus and the plants growing around about us, to illustrate this use of the "dotted" line. To achieve that essential quality of the dotted line into the forms of Taliesin West he used many small details, mostly executed in wood. Along the edges of fascia boards, for example, were placed 2″ × 2″ dentils — cubes of redwood spaced 2″ apart, running in a steady line. As the sun moves across the sky, the shadows cast by these dentils form as much a part of the architecture as the boards and cubes themselves. Shadow and the use of varying shadows becomes an important element in the overall design. The great redwood trusses that hold the canvas overhead in the Office, Drafting Room and Garden Room are also examples of a carefully planned geometry which creates shadows along the structural members themselves, as well as casting interesting patterns on the stone walls and concrete terraces above which they rise. There is little rectilinear planning in the building — slopes and prominent angles through-

の呼んでいた玉石を上部に詰め，コンクリートが表面を流れないように上でせき止めた。これが思いがけぬ効果を生むことになった。凹凸の表面をもつ石の周りを丸い小さな石が縁どり，そのラヴェンダーとグレイの色の織りなす両者のコントラストが，壁全体にわたってメロディとリズムを奏でたのであった。

ある時，フェローシップがアリゾナ北部へ遠出をした時のこと，かつては水面下にあった峡谷の壁に，水による浸蝕で水平の溝が深く刻まれていたのがライトの心にいたく印象に残ったらしい。キャンプに戻ると壁を作っている弟子に指示を与え，石積とコンクリート打ちを前に仮枠の内側に三角形断面の目地棒を付けさせた。仮枠が外された時には，壁のコンクリートに刻まれた水平の目地で，モザイクの壁に太陽が深い影をつくり，新たな要素を加えることになった。光と影というこの要素は建設の当初からタリアセン・ウェストでは一貫して考慮されて来た。

「砂漠には，きっちりとした直線は似合わない」とライトは私たちに言っていた。私たちの周りに生えているサボテンをはじめとする砂漠の植物の花を例にとって，「切れ切れの」線を使うことをそう説明した。タリアセン・ウェストの形態に点線という特性を取り入れるにあたって，ライトは数々のこまやかなディテールを駆使したが，その多くは木によるものだった。たとえば鼻隠しの上に2インチ角のデンティル（歯状装飾）を作るには，米杉の2インチ角の立方体を間隔をあけて直線に並べた。太陽が空を移動するのにつれてこのデンティルが影を落とすと，ただの板と立方体にすぎなかったものが建築全体の一部分としての生命を与えられるのだった。事務所，製図室，ガーデン・ルームを蔽うキャンヴァスを張るための米杉の大きなトラスも，構造部材，それ自身に陰影が生じると同時に，それを支える石の壁とコンクリートのテラスの表面にもおもしろいパターンを落とした。この建物には直角と直線で構成されるものは少ない。屋根勾配をはじめ主な角度も，周りの山々のそれを反映したものなのだ。

ところどころ，装飾的な頂華が壁から突き出して，キャンヴァス製のサイドフラップを留める。これが鮮やかな彩色を施されることでさらに際立っている。金色，赤，白それに青。これらキャンヴァス製のサイドフラップは何年にもわたって変化しつづけた。ある時は赤と白の布だったが，のちにそれが金色と白になった。マッシブで物静かな石の壁をあるいは横切りあるいは蔽う，この上部構造は，やはり海の水面下の世界を思わせる。梁とトラスは甲殻類の殻のように外側に出るが，その間と下には柔らかい部材，白色のキャンヴァスが張られている。

キャンヴァスが使われているために，頭上には，絶え間なく僅かな動きが繰返される。穏やかな微風が広い布に動きを伝えると，そこに静かなうねりが生じ，絶えることのない，呼吸のような頭上の動きの美しさは，それを伝える言葉を私は知らない。ここでもまたコントラストが強調されている。つまり，デリケー

out abstractly echo the angles and slopes of the surrounding mountains.

In places there are decorative finials that project out from the walls to hold canvas side flaps, and extend further in brightly painted colors: gold, red, white and blue. These canvas side flaps were likewise changed over the years — sometimes they were alternating squares of red and white, later gold and white. Across and above the massive, quiet stone walls this entire superstructure is again underwater-like: the beams and trusses are outside, like the shells of crustaceans, while in between and below is the soft membrane, in this case, the white canvas.

There was always a slight motion above because of the canvas. A gentle breeze would make the wide stretches of fabric move in a quiet billowing way, and the beauty of that ever-moving, almost breathing, overhead can never be fully described. Again — contrast: that sail-like ceiling, so delicate and perishable, riding over masses of stone and concrete. Strong windstorms gave the impression within of being on a square-rigger, upon the high seas, during a gale or squall. It was dramatic; it could sometimes be terrifying.

From the beginning of the design the three main rooms that were planned for toplighting by means of a canvas overhead were the Office, the Drafting Room, and the Garden Room. The Office, the first building that is adjacent to the car court, was the room in which Mr. Wright and his secretary-apprentice Gene Masselink worked on correspondence, manuscripts, and the general business of running the office and the school. This was also the reception area where clients and contractors met with Mr. Wright or Gene. The Drafting Room, up a few steps, is the large room in which all the architectural work was done. The Garden Room was a large living room for the Wrights, opening onto an enclosed garden, and used for Fellowship social occasions as well.

The paradox of these three spaces lies in the fact that the walls are massive, strong, almost fortress-like stone masonry, while the overhead is delicate, diaphanous, textile. For this very reason Mr. Wright continually revised, rebuilt, rearranged the textile overhead. No two photographs, taken a year apart of the same room, show the roof the same way. It was as though on a great stone masonry foundation, as a steadfast rhythm, the architect kept modifying the melody, this delicate light-filled overhead.

In the early stages, lapped boards ran down the center of the roof, then more and more canvas stretches were used, until finally the entire upper surface, turning at right angles both at the upper and lower ends of the slopes were likewise canvas that came down onto the masonry supports, set in between the redwood

トで消え入らんばかりの帆のような天井が，量感に満ちた石とコンクリートの上に浮かぶ。強風ともなれば，台風やスコールのさなか，波高い海なりをものともせず帆船で乗り出したかのようだった。ドラマティックな状況は，時として恐ろしくさえ感じられた。

設計の当初から，頭上のキャンヴァスを透かした採光は，事務所，製図室，ガーデン・ルームに計画してあった。カーポートから入って最初の部屋である事務室では，ライトが秘書を兼ねた弟子のジーン・マセリンクを従えて書類や原稿を書くほかに，事務所や学校を運営するための仕事一般を行なっていた。ここはまた，クライアントや施工業者がライトとジーンに会う応接室でもあった。数段上った位置にある広い製図室では，建築に関わる仕事がすべてなされる。ガーデン・ルームは囲われた庭に面する，ライトのリビング・ルームだが，フェローシップの社交的な催しの時にもここが使われた。

これら3つは逆説的な空間であった。壁はマッシブで力強く，さながら石の要塞のようでありながら，頭上を蔽うのは繊細で透明な布だったからだ。屋根に張った布の張り替えと建て直しをライトが繰返したのは，ほかならぬこの理由からだった。同じ部屋を一年ごとに撮った写真を比べてもひとつとして同じものはない。たとえて言えば，着実なリズムを刻む石積を基礎としながら，メロディに手を加えつづける音楽家のように，この繊細な光溢れる蔽いをライトは編曲しつづけたのだった。

最初の段階では屋根の中央に板葺が用いられていたが，次第にキャンヴァスが多くなり，結局は表面の全てを蔽い尽くし，傾斜の上下の端で直角に折れる石積の構造体まで下がるキャンヴァスが米杉のトラスからトラスへ張りわたされた。

こうした絶え間ない改造が，その都度の解決法に満足しきれなかったためなのか，それとも室内の家具ばかりでなく，天井や屋根までも手を加えられることの喜びを表わすものなのかは推測の域を出ることができない。たしかに，その前の解決の失敗が理由で改造が行なわれたこともあった。時にそれはシステムの設計上の問題が原因であり，時には材料のせいだった。いずれの場合も，使われた労働力は決して熟練したそれではなかった。弟子たちは実際に自分たちで建てることによって，建築をつくる技術を学んでいたこともあり，新しい技術を試みるのは，それが成功するにせよ失敗に終わるにせよ，これが自分自身の住まいであったからこそやれる実験なのだと，一連の試みについてライトは考えていたのである。あるものは災害という不可抗力によるものだが，あるものは構造的な，従って防ぐことの可能なはずのものだった。ライト夫人自身も，パイオニア精神を持つ人だったから，普通の人であれば耐え切れぬであろうような度重なる苦労にも，挫けることがなかった。私たち弟子の方は，まだ若く強かったから耐えられぬはずもなかったが，80代にもなる年齢の人が自らの住宅をすすんで実験台にしようと

trusses.

Whether these constant changes reflect a dissatisfaction with each solution, or whether they reflect the joy and pleasure the architect derived from being able to rearrange not only the furniture within the rooms themselves, but the ceiling and roofs as well, remains up to one's own conjecture. There were certainly times when the roof modification was expressly carried out because the prior solution was failing, due sometimes to the design of the system and sometimes the materials involved. In both cases the labor involved was anything but skilled: the apprentices themselves were learning the craft of building by building, and throughout the entire venture Mr. Wright considered the affair as an experiment which he could afford to carry on because it was his own home and he was accountable only to himself for its success or failure as new techniques were tried. Some proved disastrous, some proved structural and stayed. Mrs. Wright, possessing a pioneering spirit herself, bore with it all when many times the hardships involved would have broken lesser people. We who were the apprentices were certainly young and strong enough to endure. Certainly if a man in his 80s was willing to "experiment" in his own home, we could well pitch in with him and learn, as he was learning.

But I would hazard the guess that he did indeed derive great satisfaction from the ability to so easily alter his own work this way. Change was a vital principle in his nature, and he quoted Heraclitus, the Greek philosopher, who was stoned in the streets of Athens, some two thousand or more years ago, for stating that the only immutable, unchangeable law is the Law of Change.

When Taliesin West was first built, the Fellowship numbered about 30 people, and the structure was designed to provide shelter and living space for that group with further provisions for guests on a long deck above the loggia. The Dining Room south of the Kitchen was comfortable for the number; a spacious fireplace kept the room warm and cozy on the cold desert mornings in winter. A typical Arizona winter's day begins with a chill in the air, but by ten or eleven in the morning the sun warms up the atmosphere, and by early afternoon the canvas flaps which served in the Dining Room as narrow windows above the surrounding stone walls could be swung open to catch the breezes. By early evening, on the other hand, the flaps were closed and another fire set in the fireplace. A long loggia stretched out east from the Kitchen to the wing containing Mr. and Mrs. Wright's private living quarters: at right angles to this east/west access was the Garden Room, while the east-west direction contained kitchen, bath, two bedrooms and sitting room. The sitting room window opening — still "glazed" in canvas when first built —

していればこそ、私たちも彼と共に歯を食いしばって学ぶことができたのである。ライト自身が学ぶことをやめようとしなかったのだから。

だが、あえて推測をするなら、彼としてはこんな具合に自分の作品を気軽に変えられるということに大いに満足感を覚えていたに違いない。変化は、彼の性格のうちでも中核をなす原理だったから、「変化の法則のみが不変の理である」と説いた科で、2000年以上も昔のアテネの街で石打ちの刑に処せられたギリシアの哲学者ヘラクリトスをよく引用したものだった。

タリアセン・ウェストの建設当初、フェローシップのメンバーはおよそ30人ほどだったから、この人数を収容する宿舎とリビング・スペースのほかに、ロッジアの上の長いデッキに来客用の施設を設けてあった。厨房の南の食堂も、この人数にはほどよいものだった。砂漠の冬にむかえる朝の寒さでも大きな暖炉のおかげで部屋は暖かく心地良かった。アリゾナの冬の典型的な1日は冷たい空気とともに始まるが、朝の10時ないし11時ともなれば太陽が大気を暖めはじめ、周囲の石の壁の上にあるキャンヴァスのフラップを上げて狭い窓のような開口から風を取り入れる。けれども、夕方も早い時刻にはフラップを閉じて、また暖炉に新たな火がくべられる。厨房からライト夫妻の私室のある東ウイングまでロッジアが長く伸びていた。この東西軸には厨房、浴室、2つの寝室と談話室があったが、これに直交する形でガーデン・ルームがあった。また、はじめに建てられたときのまま、キャンヴァス張りだった談話室の窓からは見渡すかぎり、人家もない砂漠を隔ててブラック・マウンテンとグラナイト・リーフを一望することができた。この、ライト夫妻の住宅のある棟の北に広い中庭を囲んで弟子たちの宿舎が10室と一個所にまとめられた浴室があった。弟子たちの中庭が長い東西軸とぶつかる位置に、プランではホーガンとかキヴァとか呼ばれていた小劇場があった。壁から屋根に至るまで、ここはことごとく石で作られ、石の壁に深く穿たれた換気孔のほかには、暖炉があるばかりで窓がなかった。アメリカ・インディアンのホーガンやキヴァのように、ここは静謐で隔絶された印象の、洞窟のような部屋だったから、タリアセン恒例の土曜の夜のディナーと映画には格好の場所だった。寒い日にも、暖炉は部屋を暖めるに充分だったし、気候が暖かくなって来れば逆に、石積の厚い壁が室内を涼しく保つのだった。

やはり恒例だった日曜の夜の正式なディナーとコンサートは、ガーデン・ルームで行なわれた。小さな三角形のテーブルを部屋のそこここに集めて食卓をつくり、食後のコンサートは部屋の奥の、グランド・ピアノと四重奏用の台とハープのある場所で演奏された。

11年間は、小劇場としても食堂としてもこれで充分であった。けれども、戦争の終わった1946年にな

looked out across the hundreds of unpopulated desert acres to Black Mountain and Granite Reef beyond. North from this private wing, spaced around a large court, was a group of rooms for the apprentices, with bathing facilities in one area, serving the ten or more rooms. At the point where the apprentice court meets the long east-west access is the small theatre, called, on the plan, Hogan, or Kiva. A totally stone room, stone walls, stone roof, it had no window opening except for some air vents cut into the deep masonry walls, and a fireplace. Like the American Indian hogan or kiva, it was a quiet, secluded cave-like room ideal for the customary Saturday evening dinners and cinema at Taliesin. In cold weather the fireplace was sufficient to amply heat the room. When the weather got warmer the thick masonry walls kept the interior relatively cool.

The equally traditional Sunday evenings of formal dinner and musical concert were held in the Garden Room. Dinner was served on small triangular tables grouped about the room, while the concert took place after dinner at the end of the room where there was a large piano, quartet stand and harp.

The little theatre sufficed for eleven years, as did the equally small dining room. But when the war ended in 1946, more apprentices began coming from Europe, Africa and Asia, as well as more from the United States, and the Fellowship's enrollment increased from 35 to 60. At first Mr. Wright planned to expand the existing small theatre, digging the building into the ground behind the low wall along the east-west pergola and walkway. But finally, in 1948, he abandoned the idea of expansion, and instead designed another theatre, stretching out north from the office terrace in the direction of the McDowell Mountains behind camp. And the large open loggia, east of the kitchen, was enclosed to provide a larger dining room. The former one was converted into a small, private dining room where Mr. and Mrs. Wright could entertain friends and clients.

Each of the spaces at Taliesin West has its own character and its own architectural form, but all combine together into one integrated whole. It is, therefore, a building composed of many buildings linked together by terraces, walkways, courtyards. The orientation out to the southwest looks over sunken gardens, a triangular pool, and finally the prow itself. The desert foliage resembles, in many ways, the type of growth found on the ocean floors. Staghorn and Cholla cactus resemble more the strange shapes and forms of coral than the type of trees and foliage found in either temperate or tropical zones. Once again we have this analogy to the sea, and Taliesin West, with its sloping stone and concrete prow, does indeed resemble an abstract ship set afloat on this desert "sea."

ると，アメリカ国内の各地からはもとより，ヨーロッパ，アフリカ，アジアなどからやってくる弟子たちで，フェローシップのメンバーは35人から60人に膨れ上がった。そこで，ライトは既存の小劇場の拡張を計画し，東西方向のパーゴラと通路に沿い低い壁の裏に掘り込もうとした。だが1948年には，結局この拡張案をあきらめ，別に劇場を作る計画にとりかかった。キャンプの背後のマクダウェル山系に向かって開いた事務所のテラスから北の方向に作ろうというものだった。厨房の東の，広い吹き放しのロジアを閉じてここを食堂にして，もとの食堂は，ライト夫妻が友人や施主をもてなす私的な用途に使われるようになった。

タリアセン・ウェストの各々のスペースは，それぞれに独特の性格と形態を持っていたが，それら全体が結ばれて，一体となっていた。すなわち，数多くの建物がテラス，通路などによって結ばれていたのである。南西の方向に目を向ければサンクン・ガーデンと三角形のプール，それに舳先も見える。砂漠の植物は，いろいろな意味で海底の植物と似通っている。スタグホンやチョーリャなどと呼ばれるサボテンは，温帯や熱帯に生える樹木や植物よりはむしろサンゴの不思議な形態を思わせる。やはりここにも海とのアナロジーがある。タリアセン・ウェストの傾斜した石の壁やコンクリートの舳先は，文字通り砂漠の「海」に浮かぶ船のようだ。

製図室に沿って，格子に蔽われた「パーゴラ」と呼ばれる長い通路がある。建設当初，製図室の北側はこのパーゴラに向かって開放され，何も閉じるものがなかった。キャンヴァスの天井は北から南に向かって傾斜していたので，机の上には作業に望ましい，北側からの光を採り入れる高い開口があった。太陽が東から西に移動する間，そこに降り注いだ光は，キャンヴァスを美しく輝かせ，透過光となって室内を満たした。

ガーデン・ルームの高窓は東を向いていたから日の出とともに部屋は輝く光に溢れ，夕方にはキャンヴァスに照りつける光が室内を明るく黄金色に染めた。

キャンプのどの位置からでも，外に目を向ければ，一方には山々と台地の，息を呑む雄大な光景が，また中庭に目を転じれば水のはじける噴水と緑あふれる庭があった。光を反射する目的でいたる所に池が作られていたが，この池は緊急の時，つまり防火用水として，また停電の時に植物や庭に水が必要になる場合に備えてのものでもあった。

のちに，非常用として給水塔が作られた。工作室のわきの，前庭の位置には照明塔が加えられ，玄関まわりを明るくした。この照明塔は石とコンクリートによる傾斜した柱で，金属製の彫刻が一方の側に下がり，その反対側には長いスティール製のポールが伸びて投光器を支えている。これも，岩に彫

The Drafting Room flanks a long walk covered with trellises called the "pergola." When first built, the north flank of the Drafting Room opened all along its side onto this pergola, with no enclosure whatsoever. The canvas ceiling slopes from the north down to the south side, so that high bays of openings could bring in desirable north light for work at the tables, while the sun, as passing from east to west, poured onto the canvas and produced a beautiful, glowing, translucent light within.

The high side of the Garden Room was planned to look out to the east, the sun's early morning rays filling the room with sparkling light, the late afternoon sun hitting the canvas and illuminating the interior with a luscious golden light.

From within looking out, everywhere throughout the camp, were breathtaking vistas of mountains and mesas, or views into enclosed courtyards with splashing fountains and green gardens. Water — in the form of reflecting pools, was provided at various places along the plan. These pools of water served also in case of emergency — fire — or times when the electric current was off and water was needed for planting and gardens.

A water tower was later added to act as a reservoir water supply. A light tower was added at the entry court, next to the workshops, from which lights could illumine the entrance area. The Light Tower is a great sloping shaft of stone and concrete, with metal sculpture suspended along one surface, and a long steel pole extending out from the other to hold the actual flood-lights. Here again the massive masonry is a dramatic abstraction of the rock-carved world of Arizona's mountains.

The nature of Taliesin West, from its very beginning, was camp-like. Life was lived in rather primitive conditions: not too many bathrooms; electricity for all power was provided by our own diesel generator (turned on at five in the morning, and turned off at ten at night); no heating or air-conditioning; electrical wiring to a minimum that would, today, defy even the most minimal of code requirements. Those of us who lived and worked there during that first decade of its construction refer to the building as "camp," and now with all the changes and civilizing elements that have come into the building with the need to move and change with the times, we still — out of mere habit — call it "camp," to the startled amazement of newer staff and apprentices who find it quite luxurious with all the air conditioning, the telephones, the TV, the computers, etc.

And in those early years, living in this tent-like structure, we learned that the desert could be inordinately cruel. The sun could burn in the sky and parch every-

刻を施したようなアリゾナの山々の演じる世界をドラマティックに抽象化した，量感のある石積となった。

タリアセン・ウェストはその発足の当初からキャンプのような性格を持っていた。生活はいささか原始的なもので，あらゆる電気は自家発電で賄っていた（朝の5時に始動して夜の10時に停止した）。暖房も空調もない。電気の配線も最小限に抑えてあったから，今日ある最低基準すら満たしていなかった。建設開始以来のはじめの10年を生活しつつ働いた私たちは，ここを「キャンプ」と呼んでいたが，時とともに改造の必要に迫られて，この建物も大きく変貌し，文明の利器が加えられた今も，私たちは染みついた習慣からいまだにここを「キャンプ」と呼んでいるので，新しいスタッフや弟子たちは空調，電話，テレビもコンピュータも備えられた現在の状態を目にしてはいささか面喰っているようだ。

このテント式の構造物で生活を始めたころ，砂漠というものが，並々ならぬ残酷さを持つものだと身をもって知らされた。太陽が空に昇るや，光線に触れるものすべてを焦がし，一転して大嵐（砂漠の悪魔と呼ばれた）ともなれば小型のトルネードのように動きまわり地表を一掃すると，埃や小石を高く巻き上げるや，それを建物の上に落とし，キャンヴァスを木製の枠から引きちぎり，あちらこちらを隙間だらけにした。雨期には，砂漠の洪水は危険すら感じさせた。あたりの地面は，砂と岩と小石でできていたから吸水性がすこぶる悪い。どしゃ降りの雨は裏山の斜面を下り，満ちて来る海の波のように，涸れていた浅瀬を渦巻く激流に変え，その地域を横切り行く手にあるものをことごとく呑み込む。当時の私たちは，物を濡らさずにおこうという考えをはなから放棄して，床といわず屋根といわず，侵入する洪水から，せめて貴重品——大部分は図面だった——だけは護ろうと奮闘した。ある時，いつになく長い雨期が明け，嵐もおさまって雷鳴も走り去ってゆくのだと，耳に届いた音を私たちはそう思った。これが実は，北の山々を流れ落ちる水のうなりだったのである。タリアセンの下の谷を溢れさせ動力も電話も途絶え，私たちは3日間というもの文字通り孤立させられたのだった。その後ライトは建物の北に溝を掘り，押し寄せる水を建物の両脇の排水溝に導くようにさせた。

このような出来事は，すぐれてロマンティックな驚くほどの美しさを持つ建物に住む代償として私たちの耐えねばならぬ辛苦であった。けれども，嵐がおさまり，再び姿を現わすや太陽は，乾燥した暖かい空気の中で見る見るうちにあらゆるものを乾かしてしまい，ほしいままに力をふるう，手に負えぬアリゾナの環境の中でタリアセン・ウェストの生活が再開される。私たちは若く元気いっぱいだった。なにしろ，ここの建物は自分たちの手で建てたものなのだから。その中でも最も若々しかったのは，精神的にも行動のうえでもフランク・ロイド・ライトその人だった。オルジヴァンナ夫人に力づけられながら，砂漠に向う冒険の指揮をとっていたのである。季節ごとに数々の困難がやって来ても，ロマンスと美への憧憬が

thing under its rays; great wind storms — called desert devils — could sweep across the land like small fast-moving tornadoes, throwing dust and gravel high in a column that came upon the buildings and tore canvas from their wooden frames, wreaking havoc within. And during the rainy spell, the desert floods were hazardous. The soil all about is non-absorbent because of its composition of sand, rocks and gravel. Therefore the rain water, coming off the mountain slopes behind, came in torrents — like a moving tidal wave, turning the dry washes into turbulent rivers, pouring across the territory and into everything in its course. At those times we gave up all idea of keeping dry, and only tried to save valuables — mostly drawings — from the deluge coming in both from ground level and above. After one particularly long spell of raining, the storm ceased, and we could hear what we thought was distant thunder; it was the roar of the waters coming down the washes from the mountains to the north. It flooded the valley below us, cut off all power and telephone lines, and left us virtually marooned for three days. Later Mr. Wright planned deviation ditches north of the building, to direct the oncoming water across the flat lands to washes on either side of the main structure.

These were the hardships and difficult times we put up with in this remarkably romantic and startlingly beautiful building. But when the storms ceased, and when the waters receded, with the sun shining again everything dried out quickly in the warm arid air, and once more life went on at Taliesin West in this powerful and formidable Arizona environ. We were young and vigorous; we had built these buildings with our own hands, and the youngest of us all — in spirit and in action — was Frank Lloyd Wright who, with Olgivanna encouraging him, had initiated this venture onto the desert. The romance and the beauty far outweighed any of the seasonal hardships.

It was Mr. Wright's original intention that the white canvas, stretched over redwood frames, was to be placed between the roof trusses seasonally; the camp was truly to be a tent-like structure, the canvas roofs put up in place during the winter and taken down and stored during the summer when we migrated to Wisconsin. But the buildings came to be used longer and longer each subsequent season. The first treks to Arizona took place after Christmas, in late December, with the return trip taking place following Easter, or early Spring. Eventually the winter season in Arizona stretched from October to May, and the canvas — once installed — was left in place. This meant that the material was up for twelve months, exposed — the worse for the wear — to the sun's intense rays in summer. It needed constant repair and replacement. I am sure that this required need for repair and replace-

それにまさっていたのである。

米杉のフレームに白いキャンヴァスを張って，屋根のトラスに嵌め込むというのは，ライト自身の意図によるものだった。キャンプは文字通りテント式の構造で，キャンヴァスの屋根は冬の間だけ取り付け，ウィスコンシンに戻る夏の間は取り払って収納されるのだった。ところが，年とともに滞在期間が長くなっていった。はじめてのアリゾナ行きは12月，それもクリスマスのあとに出発して，翌年の春のはじめ，イースターに戻った。時としてアリゾナで過ごす冬の期間は10月から5月までに延び，キャンヴァスは一度取り付けられるとそのままになった。材料は1年12か月間にわたって灼熱の陽光にさらされることになった。そのため絶えざる補修と交換が必要になったのである。こうして修理と交換が繰り返され，季節ごとの行事と化するようになったことが，屋根構造の設計のやりなおしにかかった第一の理由に違いないと私は思う。これはライトにとって抗し難い誘惑で，毎年のように，これに屈したのだった。

1941年のはじめ，建物全体が完成して住みはじめた直後，オルジヴァンナ・ロイド・ライトはこのキャンプにガラスを使うことを検討するよう求めた。けれどもライトはこのキャンヴァス張りの屋根の実験に関してはいささかも後に引かず，妻に釘をさしてこう言った。「タリアセン・ウェストには1インチたりともガラスは使わないよ。これはテント式の建築でなければならない。ここにはガラスを入れる所などどこにもないよ。」

ある年のこと，数週間も灰色の空が続き，ついには砂漠の雨期が始まり土砂降りがやって来た。キャンプは横帆船のようにして身を護る。キャンヴァスのフラップをきっちりと下ろして吹きつける風と雨をしのぐのである。嵐は時々砂漠を通りすぎ，太陽は滅多に姿を見せなかった。この建築にはガラスが必要だという年来の持論を捨てずにいたライト夫人は，ある朝，夫にこう言った。「フランク，私は夢を見ました。あなたが，サン・テラスから舳先まで続いている長い部屋を作ったの。4面の壁のうちふたつは石積で，ほかの2面にはとても大きなガラスが入っていて，石の柱が広い間隔をおいて立っている。砂漠の方に稲妻を交えた嵐が来て，キャメルバック山の上に稲妻が走り，風で雲は渦巻いていたわ。マクダウェル山系は青くかすんで横なぐりの雨がその側面を打っている。あなたと私はガラスの中にふたりで並んで嵐を見て楽しんでいたのよ。」ライトは妻を見つめ笑いながらこう言った。「わかったよ，お母さん，キャンヴァスと一緒にガラスも使おう。」「これはほんとの話なのよ」と彼女は言い張った。「ほんとうにきのうの夜見た夢なのよ。」

「彼の決心を変えさせたのは，私がガラスを使うよう頼みつづけたからではないと思うわ。」当時を振返って彼女は言った。「あの夢の中のアイディアが彼に訴えたのだと思います。」 1945年の4月30日，

ment, almost on a seasonal basis, is most certainly one of the reasons why Frank Lloyd Wright redesigned the roof structure each time he rebuilt it. It was an incorrigible temptation for him and he succumbed to it year after year.

Beginning in 1941, right after the major portion of the entire building was up and occupied, Olgivanna Lloyd Wright asked her husband to consider putting some glass into the camp. But he was adamant about the experiment with this canvas overhead, and promptly reminded her, "Not one inch of glass is going into Taliesin West. This is a tent-like building, and glass has no place here at all!"

There was one particular season when the skies were grey for weeks on end, the desert was in its "wet" cycle, and rain poured down. The camp was secured like a square-rigger, canvas flaps tied down against driving winds and rains. Storms passed over the desert intermittently, and the sun barely shone at all. Mrs. Wright kept up her unceasing determination that the building needed some glass, and told her husband one morning, "Frank, I dreamed that you had built a long room extending from the Sun Terrace to the Point. The two walls were of solid stone, the other two were huge sheets of glass interrupted by stone piers in long intervals. There was a glittering storm in the desert — the lightning streaked over Camelback Mountain, the wind whirled the clouds. McDowell Range was blue. Diagonal lines of rain slashed its side. You and I were standing together watching and enjoying the storm." He looked at her, smiled, and said, "All right, Mother, we will use glass with the canvas." "This is the truth," she insisted. "I did have this dream last night."

"I don't think it was my constant begging him for glass that changed his mind," she recollected, "but rather the idea of the dream appealed to him." And on the same day, April 30, 1945, he wrote to the Pittsburgh Plate Glass Company " . . . The camp, when thus converted from canvas overhead to glass, will not only be a bewilderingly beautiful thing, of which we may all be justly proud, but glass will have invaded the desert spaces in a way and on a scale not seen before . . . ." Thus glass came in as skylights above, set between trusses, mitred down onto great beam ledges, along stone walls and in garden courts. The desert in all its changing states — storms, desert devils, light and dark — was a constant spectacle that could now be seen from within the buildings during colder winter weather.

In the winter of 1956-57, Mr. Wright began to effect some dramatic changes across the entire building. More glass came in, more permanent structures were added, a new theatre called the Music Pavilion; the once small locker-room at the end of the shop area was enlarged; heaters were installed; and he searched for a

彼はピッツバーグ板ガラス社にこう手紙を書いている。「……キャンプは、キャンヴァス張りをガラス張りの屋根に変えれば、驚くほど美しいものになるばかりでなく、私たちは皆それを誇らしく思うだろう。そのとき、ガラスは、いまだかつて誰も目にしたことのない方法とスケールで砂漠の中に空間を作っていることだろう。」このようにして、ガラスがやって来ると、トラスの間に嵌め込まれたスカイライトとして、途中で下に折れる梁受の部分、あるいは石の壁や中庭にと使われるようになった。おかげで、嵐や「砂漠の悪魔」、灼熱の日射から漆黒の闇へと変転極まりない砂漠の姿を、さながら終わりのないスペクタクルを観るかのようにして、寒い冬のさなかに建物の中に身を置いて眺めることができるようになったのである。

1956年から57年の冬、ライトは、建物全体に及ぶ、ある劇的な変更を加えた。ガラスが更に増えていったことのほかに、恒久的な構造物が加えられたのだ。ミュージック・パヴィリオンと呼ばれる新しい劇場である。工作室のはずれにあった小さなロッカールームが拡大された。暖房設備も設けられた。

また、彼は白いキャンヴァスに代わる屋根材料をあれこれ探したが、結果は同じ所にたどりついた。キャンヴァスの持つ性質とはいえ着実に収縮が進み、材質もますます劣化してゆく。天井に、フラップに、ドア等に使われる何千ヤードにも及ぶキャンヴァスの量を思えば、これは莫大な出費であったろう。あるとき、プラスティック系のゴムの繊維を試してみたことがあった。はじめは理想的とも思われたが、試練の季節を一度経過しただけで散々な目に遇わされることになった。暑さには縮み、寒さには伸び、伸びれば水を含み、そのうえ黴を生やしはじめるのだった。

製図室の上の大きなたるみには水が溜って、屋根勾配は水を流すには不十分で製図板の上に不気味に垂れ下がっているのを見ると、プラスティック系のゴムが伸びた様子は牛の巨大な乳房さながらのありさまだった。耳には、重さに耐えかねた木のフレームのきしむ音が聞こえ、繊維が枠の端で裂けて今にも水が製図室目がけてなだれ落ちて来るのではないかと、気が気でなかった。ライトは私たちにこう指示した。釘を使って膨らんだ部分の中央に小さな穴を開けてその下にミルクの缶を置き、水をそこに貯めろというのだった。私たちがこの材料の使用を即座にとりやめて、プラスティック系だが繊維ではない別の材料に変えたことは言うまでもない。これは1950年代中期という時代で当時プラスティックは、建築材料としてはせいぜい幼年期にさしかかったにすぎないころだったのだ。

ライトは建物をひと回りしては、タリアセン・ウェストに大変動を引き起しながら、何につけ彼の言うところの「少しでも、耐久性の向上」をはかっていたものだが、妻にこう言ったことがある。「私がここに建てたのは親指の爪ほどのスケッチに描いたものにすぎない。これを完成させるのは君の仕事だ」と。だが、彼の生涯での最後の2回ということになったアリゾナ滞在期間にも、ライトはタリアセン・ウェストの建物

roof cover that would take the place of white canvas, but produce the same results. The quality of canvas was steadily dwindling, the product getting poorer and poorer. Considering the thousands of yards of canvas for ceilings, flaps, doors, etc., this was a mounting expense. A plastic-rubber fabric was tried. It seemed ideal in the beginning, but was found to be disastrous after the first trial season: it shrunk in hot weather, expanded in cold, held rain water as it expanded, and began to mildew at the same time.

The large bays of it over the Drafting Room would fill with the water not draining off on the slope, but hanging precariously over our drafting tables as we watched the plastic-rubber stretch and sag, like great udders. We could hear the wood frames creaking under the pressure of extended weight, and fearing that the fabric would tear itself from the frames at the edges and dump an avalanche of water into the Drafting Room at each bay, Mr. Wright instructed us to puncture — with a nail — a small hole in the center of each bulging section, place a milkcan beneath, and let the trapped water drain into the cans. Of course we immediately gave up the use of this material and turned to others — in the plastic family, but not fabric. This was still in the mid 1950s, and plastics were, at that time, in a stage of infancy when it came to building materials.

As he went around the buildings effecting more drastic changes to Taliesin West, making everything what he called "more or less more permanent," he told his wife, "What I have built here is but a thumbnail sketch; it is up to you to complete it." But during the Arizona seasons of the last two years of his life he himself began to instigate a more permanent, less camp-like quality throughout the buildings at Taliesin West. It seemed that in doing so, he was fulfilling a promise, a prediction, he had made ten years earlier.

Marya Lilien, Taliesin apprentice from the very early years of the Fellowship, came to Taliesin as an architect from Poland, and went with the Wrights and fellows on their first trip to Arizona to stay at the Hacienda, in Chandler. There they worked on the models for the Broadacre City, the main large model of the city itself and the other related models of individual structures. The next year she recollected that when Mr. Wright returned from a lecture tour, he brought back one thousand dollars in cash — a great deal of money at that time — and said, "Boys, we are going to buy land in Paradise Valley — near Phoenix, and build ourselves a winter headquarters." Marya witnessed a winter in Wisconsin, and said that it was unbearably cold most of the time. The thought of going into sunny Arizona was a welcome relief for all of them. In the subsequent winters, when

の質をより恒久的なものに，できるだけキャンプのような一時的なものでなくさせようという仕事を続けていた。こうすることで，彼は10年前にしたある約束，あるいは予言を果たそうとしているかのようだった。

マリア・リリアンはフェローシップのごく初期の時代からの弟子で，ポーランドから建築家としてタリアセンに来た人だったが，彼女はライトや仲間たちと共にチャンドラーのハシエンダへの初めてのアリゾナ移動にも加わっていた。そこで彼らはブロードエーカー・シティ計画の，シティ本体の大きな模型とその他の関わりのある建物などの模型作りをしたのだった。彼女の記憶ではその翌年，ライトが講演旅行から1,000ドルほどの現金——当時にすれば相当の大金——を手に戻ると，こう言った。「諸君，フェニックスの近くのパラダイス・ヴァレーに土地を買うことにした。そこに自分たちで冬用の拠点を作るんだよ。」マリアはウィスコンシンの冬の信じがたいほどの寒さを思い浮べながらそう語った。陽光に満ちたアリゾナへ行くというのは，思うだけでも彼らのだれにとっても待望の救いだったのである。それ以後の冬，タリアセン・ウェストの工事が実行に移されたが，マリアはポーランドの家族のもとへ帰り，ナチ時代の侵略の苦悩と恐怖を身をもって体験することになった。「火事と空襲と死に囲まれながら都市が灰になり果ててゆく中で生活していると，朝になって目を覚まし，この混乱と破壊の中でまだ生命があったのを確かめるたびに奇跡のように思われました。」彼女は，家族とともに国外への脱出に成功し，ライ

ト夫妻の尽力でアメリカに渡り，シカゴのアート・インスティテュートでの教職を得ることができた。戦争が終わると，彼女はタリアセン・ウェストに招かれた。フェニックスに飛び，当時はほとんど住む人もない砂漠を車に乗せられて，タリアセンに着いた。「ライトさんはご自分が先に立って，建物をあちらこちら，部屋から部屋へ，テラスからテラスへと案内して下さいました。屋根はすべてキャンヴァスでした。もちろん石は別として，ドアや囲いも全てキャンヴァスのフラップを使ってありました。あれは，ドラマティックで美しい大規模なテントでした。ところが，急に上のキャンヴァスと米杉の梁を指さしてこうおっしゃったのよ，『これは一時的なものにすぎないんだ。10年くらいのうちにはもっと耐久性のあるガラスなどを使うようになるだろう。きっと立派なものになるよ。見ていてごらんマリア。』私を驚かせたのは，目の前にいる人物が，77歳という高齢でありながら87歳になったときに自分のすることを計画しているということでした。いかにも気づかわしげに10年後の時のことを思っていらしたのですから。」

外から見てもっとも顕著な変化は，アプローチの道路の方向であった。はじめは，敷地を横切って北から南に向って走る排水溝に沿っていた。（干上った谷や小川などの自然の地形に逆らって進もうとする道は，ひとたび大雨に見舞われれば排水溝は山を流れ落ちた水で渦巻く激流と化するのである。）そこから方向を転じて遠ざかり，建物の西端のカー・コートに入ってゆくのだった。だが，1959年

Taliesin West was actually under construction, Marya returned to her family in Poland, and went through the anguish and horrors of the Nazi invasion. "Burning, bombing, death all around us, the city crumbling into ashes, each morning awakening to the miracle of being alive in all this chaos and destruction." She was able to get out of Poland with her family, and eventually, through the help of Mr. and Mrs. Wright, to the United States where she took a teaching position at Chicago's Art Institute. When the war ended, she was invited to come down to Taliesin West. She flew to Phoenix and was driven out across the then mostly uninhabited desert to Taliesin West. "Mr. Wright himself showed me around the buildings, taking me from room to room and terrace to terrace. All the roofs were canvas, the doors and enclosures — other than stone — were canvas flaps. It was dramatic and beautiful, this great architectural tent. But suddenly he pointed up to the canvas and redwood beams and said, 'This is only temporary. In about ten years' time there will be glass, more permanent materials. It will be magnificent. Just you wait and see, Marya!' What amazed me was here, before me, was a man of 77 years planning on what he was certain he would be doing when he reached 87. He was, in fact, anxiously looking forward to it!"

From the outside, one of the most drastic changes was the direction of the approaching road. In the beginning it followed the curve of the main wash running from north to south across the property (he knew that any road that tried to go against the natural topography of this dry arroyo or small river would be washed out after the first heavy rain when the wash turns into a rushing vortex of water run-off from the mountains), and then swung far out and came into the car court at the west end of the building. But in 1959 he asked that some of the apprentices follow him with a ball of twine and some stakes for marking a new road. He and his wife walked straight out amongst the desert foliage, parallel to the southwest wall of the terrace-prow. At a certain point beyond the prow, they turned and wove their way back to the original course of the old road. This new straight section he planned as a double road, with a planted median running the full length, terminating in a stone planting area with a tall, sculptural rock set up on edge, like a stele. Now, driving up to Taliesin West, the visitor is greeted by this imposing stone mass, and rides along the double road with a full view of the buildings close by.

The buildings changed annually, as Mr. Wright saw better and better ways to alter and improve them, and as our own life conditions changed, as time changes, as all things are moving constantly and never remain static. After his death, his widow fulfilled her husband's wish to complete and expand, according to his master

のこと彼は数人の弟子に水糸を入れたボウル，杭を持たせて外に出ると新しい道路づくりにかかろうとした。夫妻は砂漠の植物の中をテラスの舳先の南西の壁に平行に，まっすぐに進んだ。舳先のずっと先のある地点でふたりは振り向くと元の道路のコースに戻る道をたどった。この直線部分には植栽による中央分離帯が付けられ，往復二車線の道路として計画された。先端には石碑のように丈高く，彫刻的な岩を据え付けた石組が設けられた。これで，タリアセン・ウェストを目指す訪問者はこの堂々たる石の塊に迎えられ，二車線の道路を走りながら間近に迫って建物を視界いっぱいにとらえるようになったのである。

建物は毎年のように変わっていった。よりよく変える方法を求めてライトが知恵をしぼるたびに私たちの生活形態は変わり，時の流れとともにあらゆる物が常に変化し，じっとしていることがなかった。ライトの死後，未亡人は，亡夫の願いを叶えるために，また，生活の変化にとっては，フレキシブルな平面がいかに必要であるかを彼女自身も知っていたので，マスタープランの通りに完成するべく拡張を試み続けた亡夫の夢を実現しようとした。タリアセン・ウェストを博物館にしようと考えられたことは，一度としてなかったけれども，日ごとに来訪者は増加の一途をたどっている。建物が建てられてからというもの，それを見るために砂漠を越えて多くの人々がやって来るようになっていたのである。年々，周囲の砂漠地帯は減少し，引き裂かれ，あるいは平らに均されディベロッパーの手で完全に荒廃させられ，旅行者の数ばかりが増えてゆく。タリアセン・ウェストの役割は50年前の時代もそうであったように，建築家の冬の拠点となることであり，建築事務所でありフランク・ロイド・ライト・ファウンデーションの資料保管所となることである。そこに住む人間の生活を持続させ支えることが，すなわち生きている人間のための生きた建築を護ることであって，死体と化した過去のモニュメントを残すことではない。

文明から孤絶し，周囲は見渡すかぎり家もハイウェイも視界を遮るものはなく，いたるところ無限という感覚に満ちていたころの，初期のタリアセン・ウェストの建設の様子を伝えるには建築家自身のことばにしくものはない。

「至上を目指すことは，疲れることであると同様に，多くは退屈なものだ。けれども，私たちは長年にわたって至高を目指して生活し，身体を動かし，生きて来たが，決して倦むことを知らなかった。」

「オルジヴァンナに言わせれば，タリアセン・ウェストは新らしく建設したというよりも，発掘されたものみたいだと言う。」

「私たちの砂漠キャンプは，あたかも天地創造の時からそこに建っていたかのようにアリゾナの砂漠に馴染んでいた。また，タリアセン・ウェストは，35人に及ぶ若い男女が7年間にわたる冬の季節に，

plan — and with her own knowledge of how life's changes demand a flexible building plan. Taliesin West was never intended to be a museum. It is on tour to the public on a daily basis, because the public has come out over the desert, ever since the building was first built, to see it. As the years go by, and the desert areas around us dwindle — torn apart, leveled out, and completely devastated by developers — the touring public is ever increasing. But the role of Taliesin West is, as it was over fifty years ago, to be the winter headquarters of an architectural school, an architectural firm and The Frank Lloyd Wright Foundation archives. To sustain and support the people who live in it, it will always remain a living structure for living people, never a dead monument to the past.

The architect's own words aptly describe the experience of building Taliesin West in those first years when the desert was isolated, the vistas all around were unimpeded by housing and highways, and the sense of the Infinite prevailed everywhere:

"Superlatives are exhausting and usually a bore — but we lived, moved and had our being in superlatives for years. Never bored.

"Olgivanna said the whole opus looked like something we had not been building but excavating.

"Our new desert camp belonged to the Arizona desert as though it had stood there during creation. And also built into Taliesin West is the best in strong young lives of about thirty-five young men and women during the winter seasons for about seven years. Some local labor went in to, but not much. The constant supervision of an architect — myself, Olgivanna inspiring and working with us all, working as hard as I — all living a full life, almost too full, meanwhile.

"The Arizona camp is something one can't describe, just doesn't care to talk much about. Something sacred in respect to excellence."

Taliesin West, even to this day with all the new and modern "improvements" that have come on the scene since it was first built as a primitive campsite, still has the presence of this sense of powerful, rugged drama. Antiquity and modernity are hand in hand at Taliesin West and Time seems to have come to a halt. It produces an aura, a magic, an atmosphere that never ceases to grip those of us who live in it on a daily basis, and even more startling to those who come upon it and experience it for the first time.

In 1949, Fowler McCormick, friend and neighbor to the Wrights in Paradise Valley, came out for dinner one evening, and later sent Mr. Wright a note thanking him for the occasion and expressing his thrill in experiencing the buildings.

その力強く若い生命力を精一杯そそぎ込んで建てられたものだ。現地の労働力にも多少は頼りはしたが、決して多くはなかった。ひとりの建築家——私のことだが——が常に目を光らせ、オルジヴァンナも皆を力づけたり励ましたりしながら私たちと共に、私と同じように働いた。だれもが力のかぎりに生きた、いや、力の限界を越えるまでと言うべきかもしれない。」

「アリゾナのキャンプは、ことばに表しがたいものがある。余り多くを語りたいと思わせない。もはや神聖なものの域に達しているからなのだ。」

タリアセン・ウェストは、はじめに、素朴なキャンプサイトとして作られて以来、数々の新しい近代的な「改良」も加えられながら今日に至ったが、それでも、困難に直面しても屈しない力強いドラマが、ここには今も生き続けている。タリアセン・ウェストでは、旧いものと新しいものが手をたずさえ、あたかも時がその歩みを停めたかのようだ。アウラと言おうか、不思議な空気を生んで、日々そこで生活する私たちを把えて離そうとしないし、はじめてここを訪ねて体験する人にとっては、それが驚きの対象となるのだ。

1949年のこと、ライトの友人で、パラダイス・ヴァレーに住んでいたファウラー・マコーミックはタリアセン・ウェストで夕食を共にした。後日、ライトに礼状を送った彼は、この建物を体験させてもらったことを感謝するとともに、その時にスリルすら感じたと書いた。それに対しライトはこう書き送った。

「親愛なるファウラーさん、

丁重なお便り有難うございました。……あなたが感じとられた通り、タリアセン・ウェストには原始と通じるものがあります。古代、人間は、幼い児が母に対してするように自然を身近にして生きていました。彼らは自ずと自然の魂を吹込まれ、どう接するべきかを教えられたのです。選択などということは思いもしませんでした。

科学や、いわゆる教育によって知的な洗練を受け、人間は素朴な幼時期から乳離れしました。いまや人類に必要なのは、さながら退化するように生物としてのあるべき姿に意識的に回帰することです。……その文字通りの意味だけでなく、象徴的な理解をして感じとることで、自然に還るということなのです。

ファウラーさん、とはいえ、タリアセン・ウェストは、未開人たちの作ったもののように単純なものでなく、より高くかつ深い理解にもとづいて作られていますから、彼らの形態を写しとったものではなく、彼らがそれと知らずに汲みとって喉をうるおした知恵の泉を私たちが探りあてて飲んだ結果なのです。そこで生まれたものは模倣ではなく根を同じくするインスピレーションでした。知を備え、実行にあたってはより多くの手段を手にした現代の私たちは、かつて幼な児のような素朴な反応しか存在しなかったところに、シ

Mr. Wright replied to him:

"Dear Fowler:

"Replying to your kind note . . . . You are perfectly right in feeling the primitive in Taliesin West. In the ancient days of the race men were close to nature as a child to its mother. They were naturally inspired and taught by her forms. They had no choice.

"Sophistication came with Science and what we call education to wean or warp them away from the simplicity of that childhood.

"Now, Mankind, as degeneracy looms, needs the refreshment afforded by a conscious return to the verities of being — returning to Nature not only in that obvious sense but with more prophetic understanding and appreciation.

"Well, Fowler — Taliesin West is modeled with that higher understanding — deeper than the simplicity of the barbarian, not copying his forms but drinking understanding from the springs from which he drank unconsciously. The result is not imitation but inspiration from the same source — now enlightened and furnished in action with more ample means to create symphony where before only the natural response of the child existed.

"Modern art feels the need of the inner strength that comes from this eternal inspiration. But, being weak falls into imitation instead of creation. Of this imitation Taliesin is not guilty.

"Taliesin West is as original as the Maya but far beyond it. More natural to environment and our life in that desert than the barbarian could have been in his time and consciously proud of it in this time.

"But we shouldn't be too proud? Or we fall."

Bruce Brooks Pfeiffer　　　　　　　　　　　　　　　　Taliesin West July 8, 1988

ンフォニーを作りあげることができたのです。

モダンアートはこの汲めど尽きせぬインスピレーションの生む内的な強さを必要としています。仮に，もしそれが弱ければ，創造ならぬ模倣に堕するのです。このような模倣は，タリアセンでは決して行なわれません。

タリアセンは，マヤ文明と同等の独自性を持っています。かつての未開人たち以上に周囲の環境に対して，さらに砂漠での生活に対して私たちは自然に振舞って来たし，そのことを，今でははっきりと誇りに思っているのです。

しかし，私たちは決して驕慢の世界に足を踏み入れてはなりません。さもなくば，たちどころの転落が私たちを待ち受けているでしょう。」

ブルース・ブルックス・ファイファー　　　　タリアセン・ウェストにて　1988年7月8日

"Ocotilla," Desert Compound and Studio, near Chandler, Arizona, 1928

"The one-two triangle," Frank Lloyd Wright wrote about his desert camp near the intended site of San Marcos-in-the-Desert, "we used in planning the camp is made by the mountain ranges around about the site. And the one-two triangle is the cross section of the talus at their bases. This triangle is reflected in the general forms of all the cabins as well as the general plan. We will paint the canvas triangles in the eccentric gables, scarlet. The red triangular form in the treatment is why we called the camp Ocotilla. Candle flame."

Ocotilla is also the name of a desert cactus that grew in the region of this camp. The structure was begun in January of 1929 and completed within six weeks. The general contour of the plan follows the contour of the small hill around which the camp spread. A zigzag wall of board, one board thick, connects all the cabins and protects the compound against snakes. Alongside of the top board of this wall ran the wiring from the electric plant in the wash below. By May of the same year, the working drawings for the hotel project were complete, and the heat of the desert summer forced the Wrights and their studio staff to abandon Ocotilla. A caretaker was put in charge of the building, pending their return next fall when construction would begin on the hotel. But the stock market crash, that October, sealed the fate of San Marcos, and of Ocotilla as well.

オコティラ

ライトは，サン・マルコス・イン・デ・デザートの建設予定地の近くに設けたキャンプについてこう書いている。「このキャンプの計画にあたって，私達は1:2の辺長比を持つ三角形を基本図形として用いたが，これは敷地周辺の山岳地帯がもとになっていた。1:2の辺長比の三角形は，足元の斜面の断面の形だったのである。これは全体の平面計画をはじめとして，さまざまな部分の形態に使われた。私達は真赤なペンキなどを塗って，キャンバスを張った三角形の裏面をちょっと派手な色にしようと思う。この紅の三角形こそ，実はこのキャンプにオコティラと名付けた理由だった。オコティラとはろうそくの炎を意味するからである。」

オコティラとはまた，このキャンプのある一帯に自生するサボテンの名称でもある。工事は1929年1月に始められ6週間で完成した。キャンプは周囲の丘陵の等高線に沿って配慮された。ボード一枚の厚さの壁がジグザグを描きながらキャビンを結びつつ蛇の侵入を防ぐ防禦壁となった。この壁の上端には，丘の下にある川床の脇におかれた発電機からの電線を這わせた。この歳の5月にはホテルの計画をすでに実施図面まで感性させながら，砂漠の苛酷な暑さのためにライトとそのスタジオのスタッフはオコティラを離れることになった。秋になってホテルの工事が始まり彼等が戻るまで，建物は管理人に委ねられることになった。ところが，この年の10月に起こった株の大暴落はサン・マルコスの命運半ばにしてその前途を閉ざした。無論，オコティラにも同じ運命が訪れたのだった。

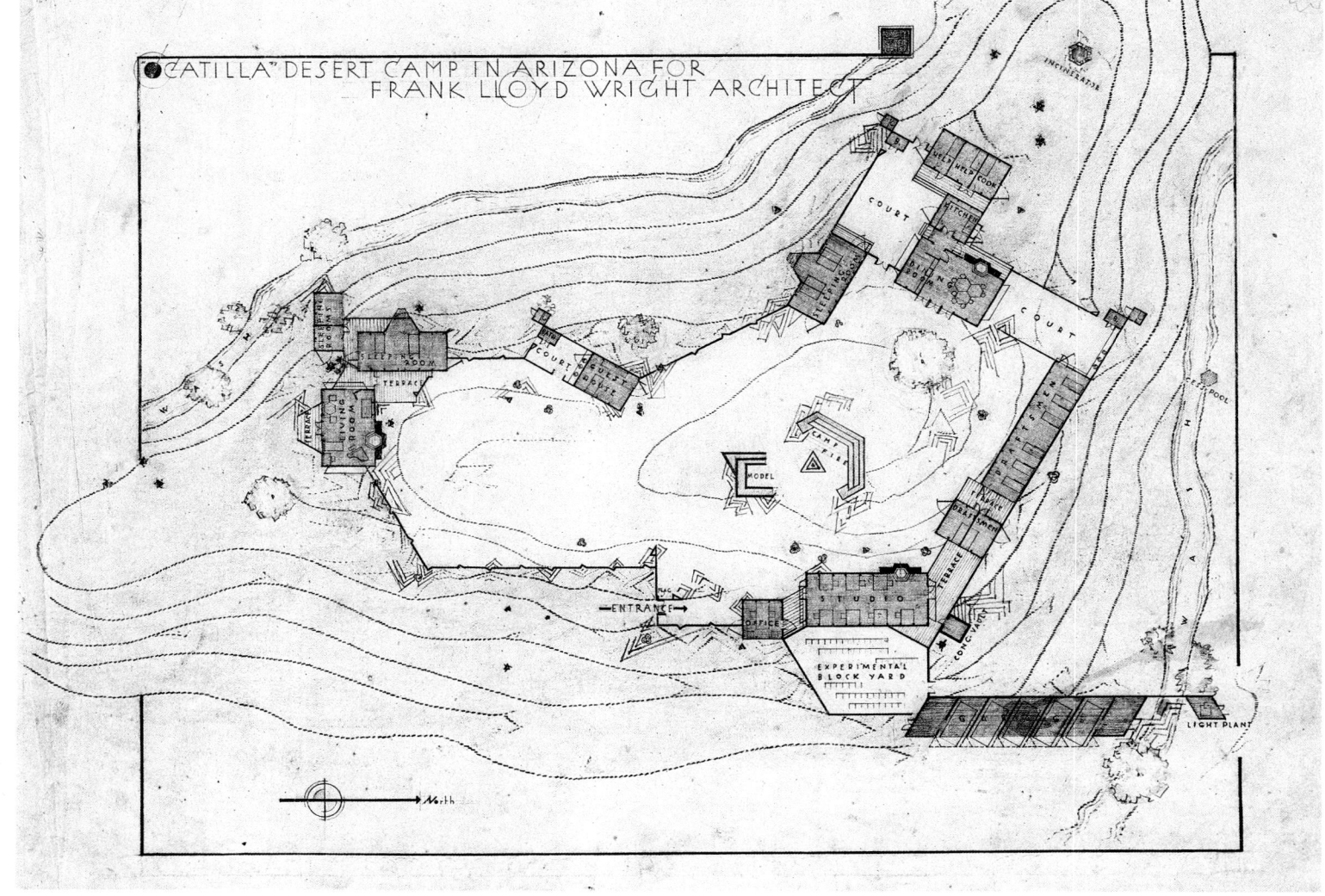

*Plot plan.*

*Construction completed March 15, 1929.*

*pp.25-49 Photographs are provided by The Frank Lloyd Wright Foundation, except as noted.*

*Construction completed March 15, 1929.*

*In construction January 30, 1929. Looking toward Wrights' living room, bedroom section completed at left.*

*In construction February 18, 1929. Looking up the hill toward drafting room and draftsmen's living quarters.*

*In construction February 1, 1929. Looking toward kitchen and dining room.*

Construction completed March 15, 1929. Architect's office at right.

The Wrights' living room, Lloyd Wright at piano. March, 1929.

Drafting room, February 12, 1929.

Sun Trap, Temporary Residence, Taliesin West, Scottsdale, Arizona, 1937

Mr. Wright designed a shelter for himself, his wife, and his daughter Iovanna. It began with a group of what he called "sleeping boxes," simple wood and canvas structures with room for a bed and small closet in each box. Living in general was consigned to the out of doors, under the warm winter sun. A stone fireplace mass provided heat from wood fires during the cold desert nights, and a small privy was set at one corner, surrounded and hidden by fast-growing oleander bushes. Gradually he expanded the structure, finally roofing it with boards and canvas throughout, with trellises at certain points along the plan. But by the time that he and Mrs. Wright had moved into new quarters at Taliesin West, a few hundred feet away, he then remodelled the "Sun Trap" into a residence for his daughter Iovanna, and the new remodelling was called, simply, the "Sun Cottage." The cottage also provided spacious accommodations for guests, since the existing "Guest Deck" above the loggia only provided small canvas cubicles. In 1960 the Sun Cottage was rebuilt in more durable materials, using steel and plastic in place of boards and canvas.

サン・トラップ

ライトは自分たち夫婦と娘のイオヴァンナのためのシェルターを設計した。はじめは木材とキャンバスで作られた単純な構造の箱の集合であった。それぞれがベッドひとつと小さなクロゼットを備えた部屋で、ライトはそれを「スリーピング・ボックス」と呼んだ。冬の暖かい陽射しのもとでの生活はおおかた自然のままに委ねられ、冷え込みの厳しい砂漠の夜は薪をくべた石積の暖炉で暖をとるのだった。一端には、成長の早い夾竹桃を周囲に植え込んだ屋外便所がもうけられた。ライトはこのボックスをつぎつぎと増やしてゆき、ボードとキャンバスを使ってそれに屋根をかけ、計画によってところどころ格子を加えた。だが、夫妻が数百フィート離れたタリアセン・ウェストの新しい一画に移ると、ライトはこの「サン・トラップ」を娘イオヴァンナの住居に作りかえて、新たにそれを「サン・コテージ」と名づけた。このコテージには広々とした来訪者用の施設も設けられた。ロッジアの上に作られていたそれまでの「ゲスト・デッキ」と呼ばれたキャンバスの立方体は小さすぎたからである。1960年になってサン・コテージは、のボードとキャンバスに代えて鉄やプラスティックなどの耐久性のある材料を用いて作り直された。

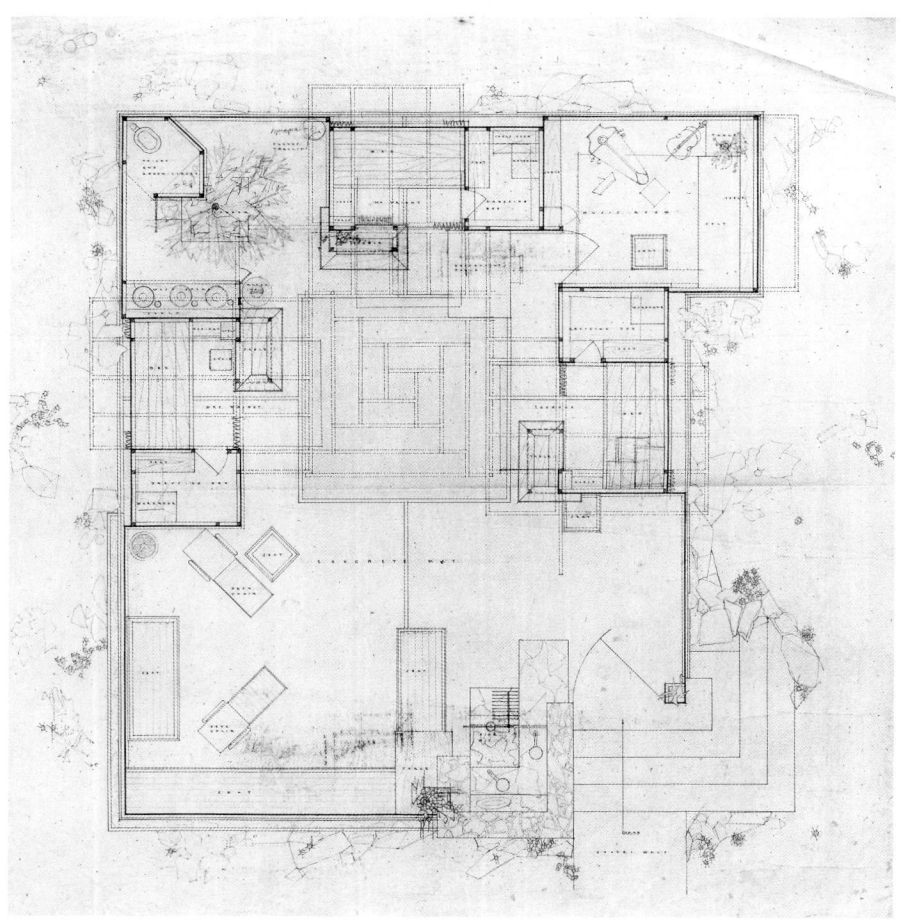

*Plan.*

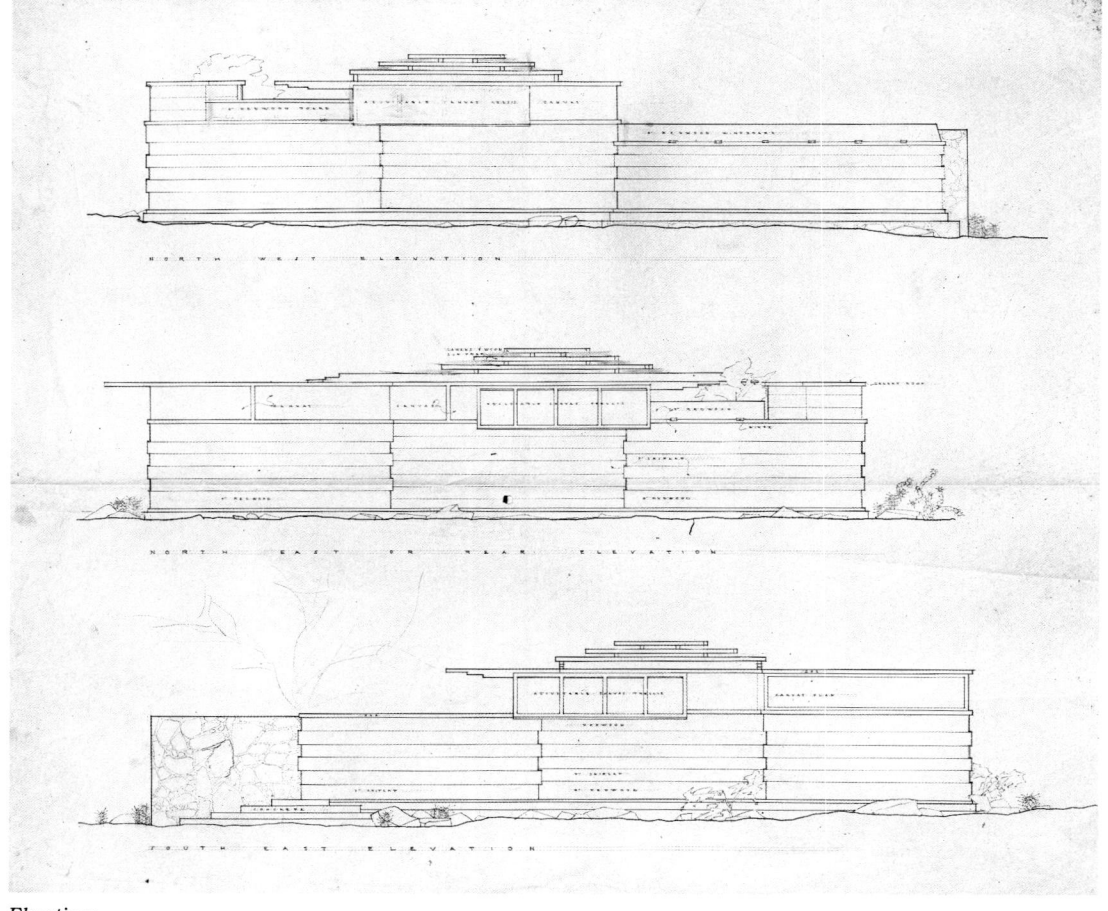

*Elevations.*

*The Wrights' temporary living quarters, 1938-39.*

*Section.*  *Section.*

*Mr. Wright supervising the moving and planting of a giant saguaro cactus, 1940.*

*Apprentices pouring concrete and masonry walls, 1947. (Photo: P. E. Guerrero)*

*View of the west end of Drafting Room to the left, Garden Room to the right, 1941. (Photo: P. E. Guerrero)*

*Stretching canvas on frames for Drafting Room roof, 1945.*

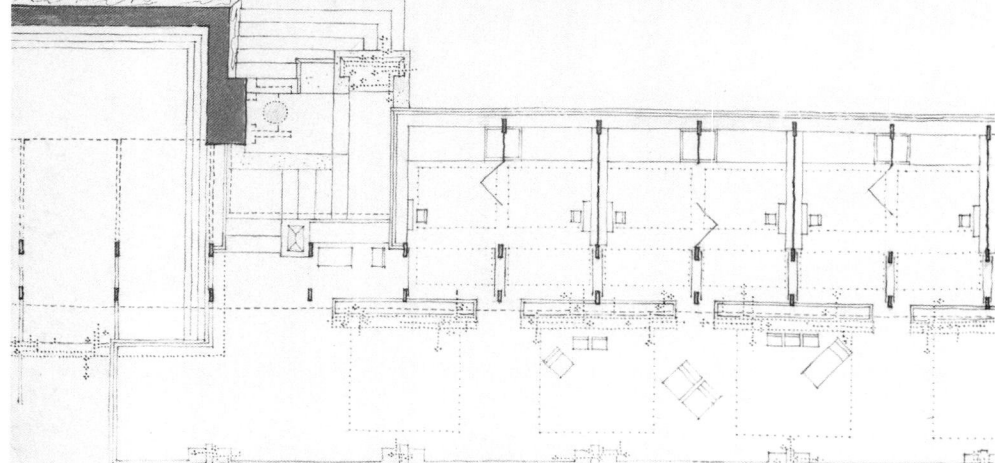

*Drafting Room roof, 1946. Plan of Guest Deck.*

*Triangular pool and dining room, 1946.*

*Drafting Room interior, 1946.*

*Loggia, 1946. Later enclosed and converted (1950) to Dining Room.*

*Loggia, 1946.*

*Loggia, Guest Deck on upper level, Bell Tower and Kitchen masonry walls beyond, 1942. (Photo: P. E. Guerrero)*

*Garden Room from enclosed garden, 1946.*

*Terrace of Garden Room, 1946.*

*Garden Room interior, 1940.*

*Garden Room interior, 1947. (Photo: P. E. Guerrero)*

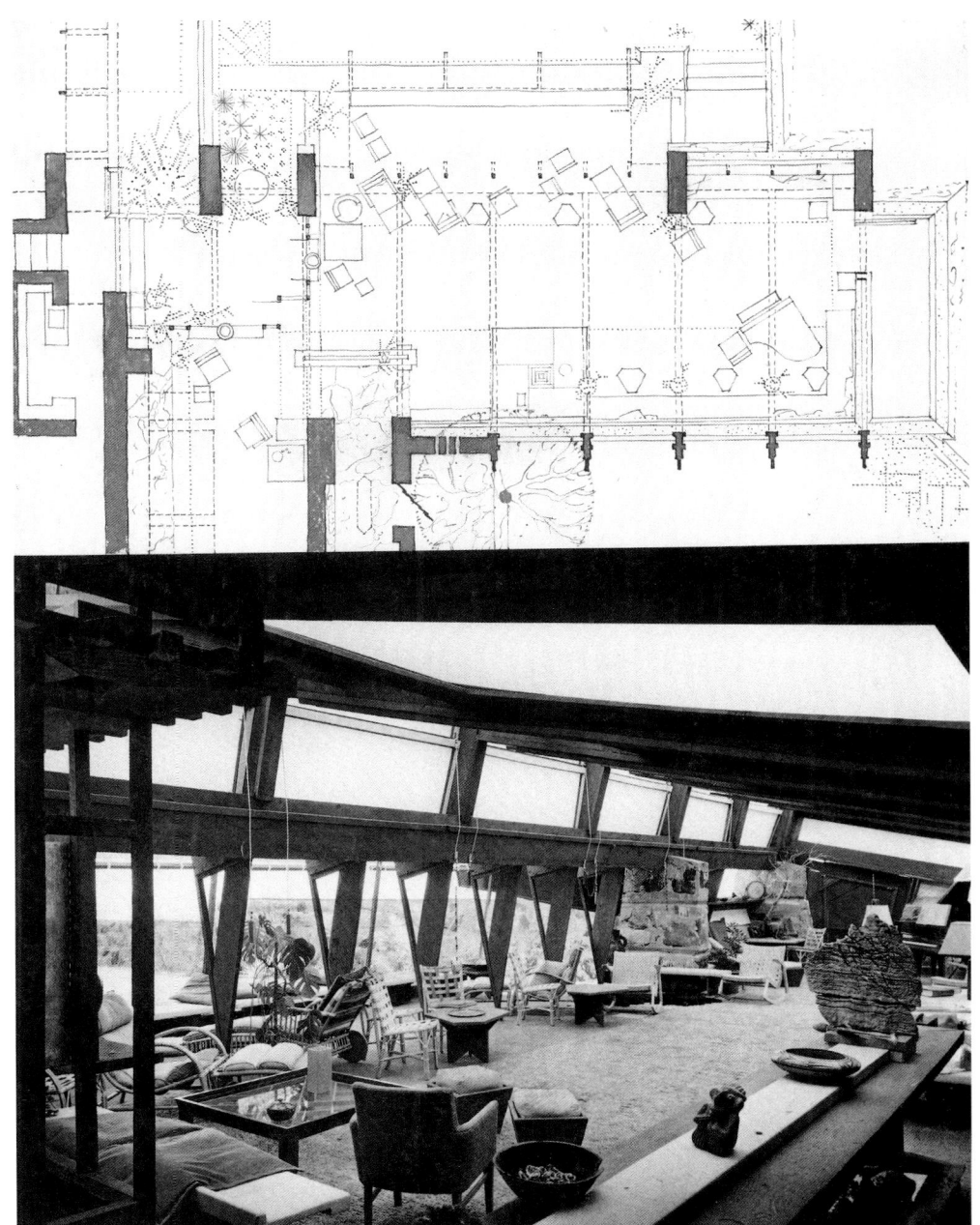

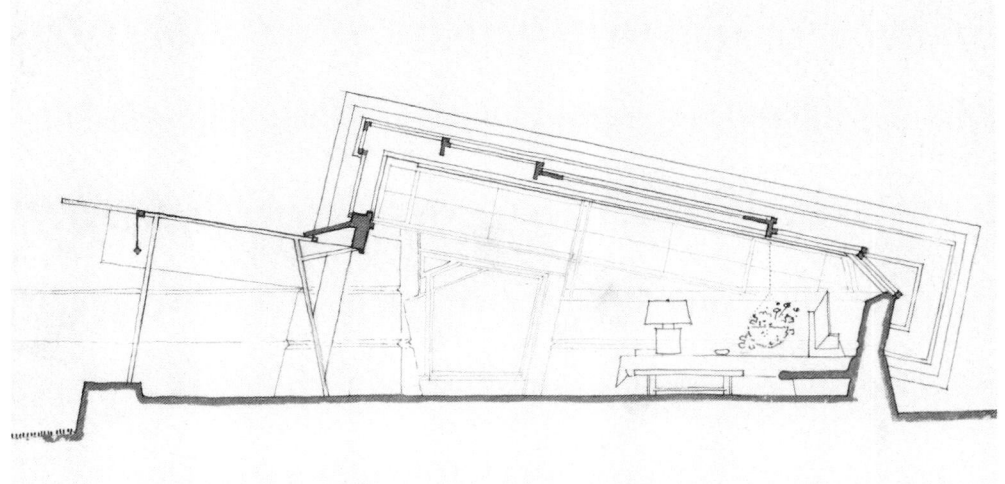

*Garden Room interior, 1946.*

*Garden Room interior, looking into Cove, 1941. (Photo: P. E. Guerrero)*

*Garden Room door looking out to Sunset Terrace, 1946.*

*Garden Room roof seen from Guest Deck, 1946.*

*Wesley Peters and Eugene Masselink living quarters, 1946.*

*Entrance to Kiva (theatre), 1946.*

*Kitchen (Galley), 1946.*

*Air view, 1959. (Photo: P. E. Guerrero)*

*View from mountain behind Taliesin West, 1959. (Photo: P. E. Guerrero)*

*Drafting Room and pool, 1959. (Photo: P. E. Guerrero)*

*Giant saguaro cactuses*

*Taliesin West sign. The design for the sign underwent many revisions until this finally evolved and was mounted in 1953.*

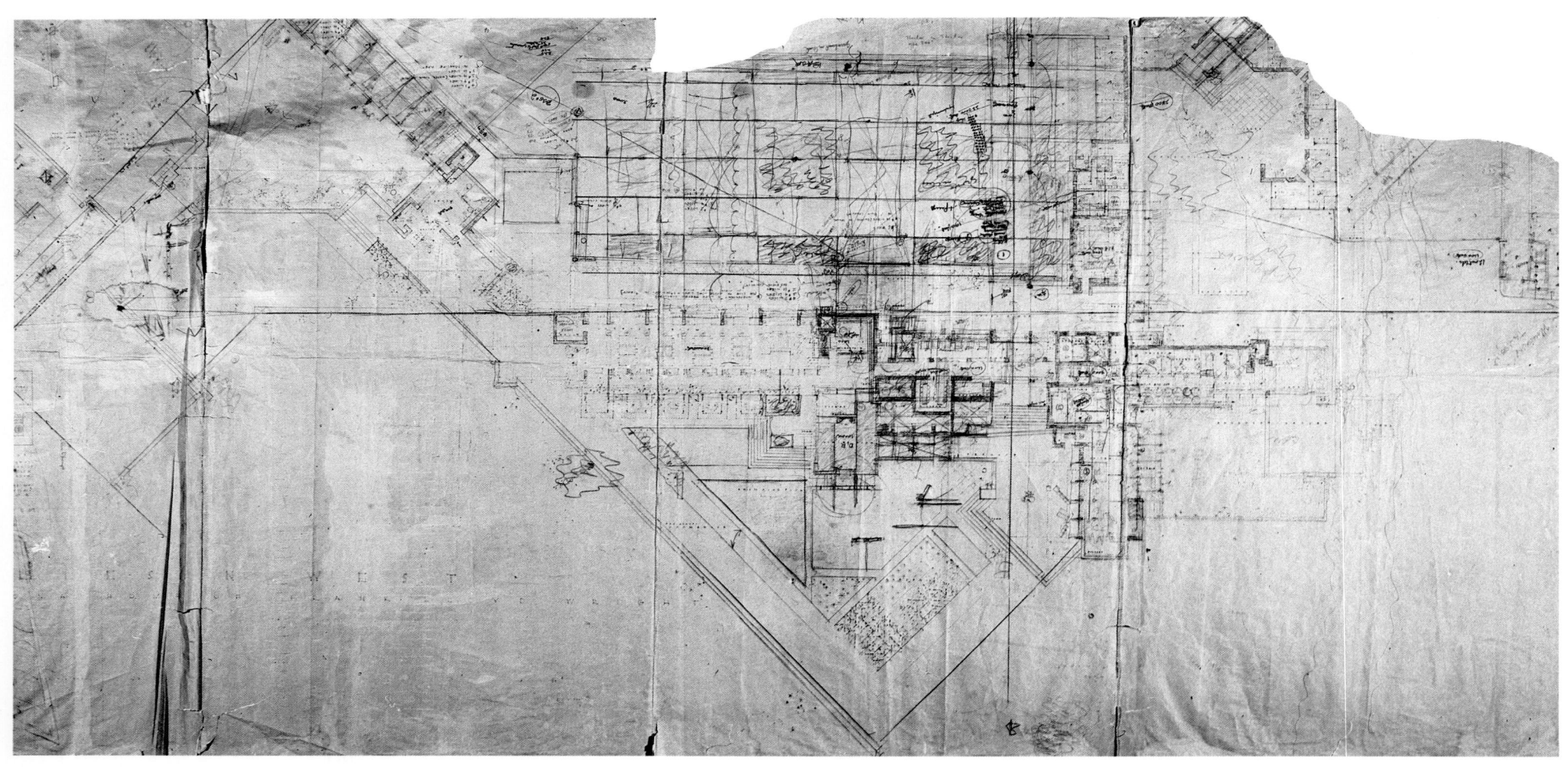

*Original master plan (concept sketch).*

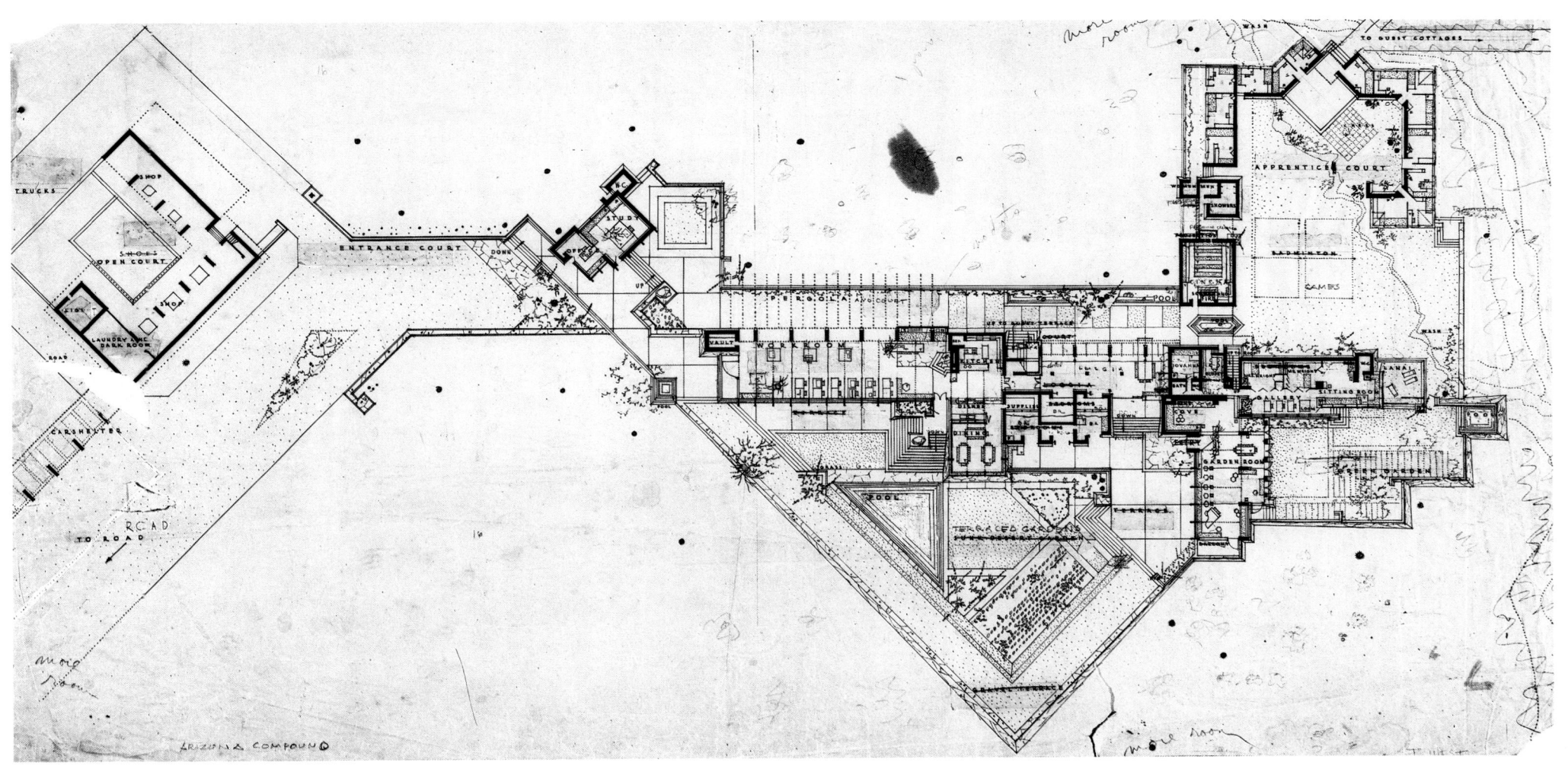

*Master plan.*

*Perspective.*

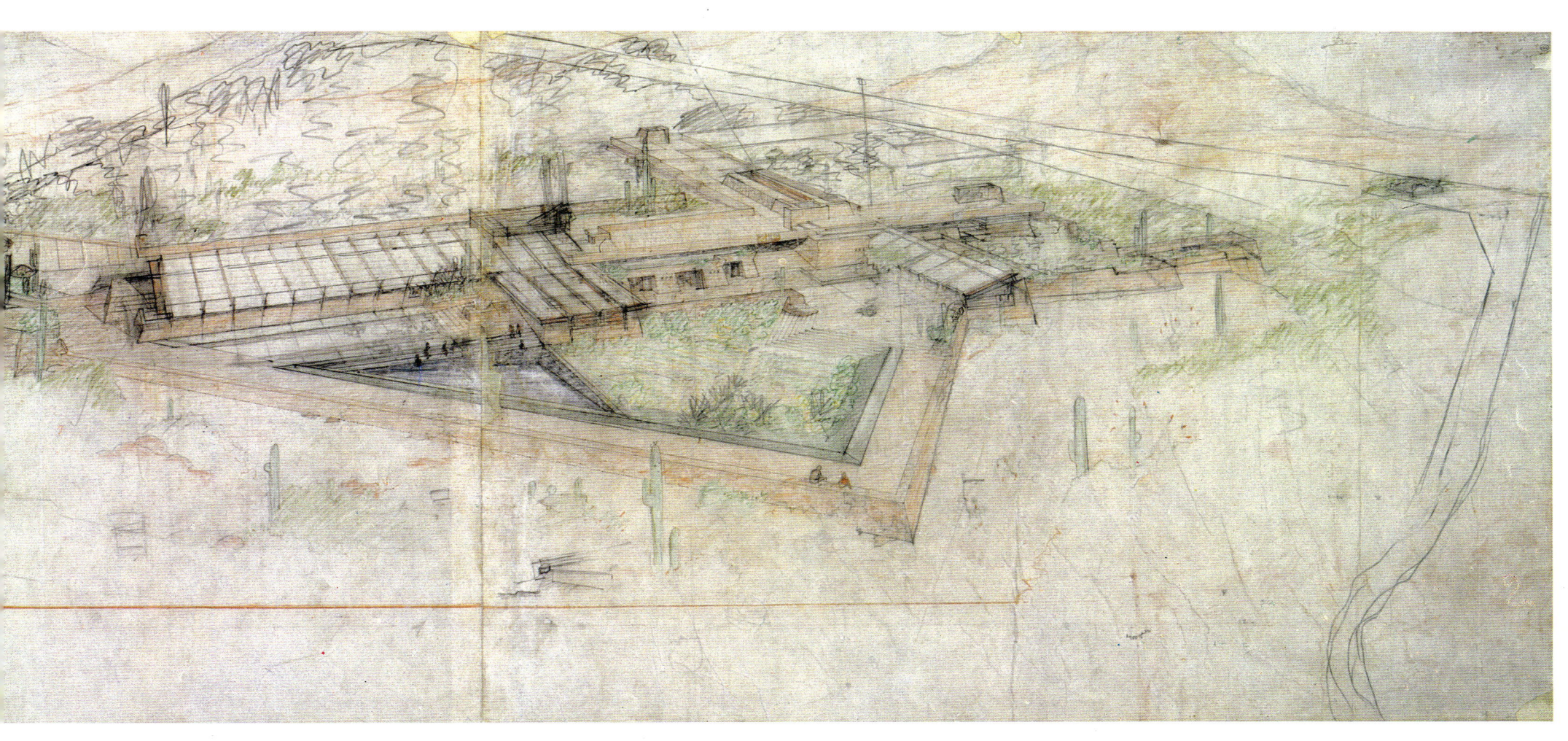

*Air view. McDowell Mountain Range in the background.*

*Air view.*

*General view from south.*

Barrel cactus

*Stele-like rock set up on edge of stone entry drive median planting area.*

*Light Tower (1947) and entry court.*

*Light Tower, fountain basin added in 1955.*

*Entrance by Office, Drafting Room beyond. Chinese Theatre (Ching) purchased as part of a group of 12, by FLLW in 1950. Midway Gardens figure and light finial brought from Wisconsin and installed in 1966, polychrome added later, in accordance with original drawings of 1913.*

*Office, to the left, Drafting Room, right.*

*Office.*

*Office, roof of Music Pavilion in the background.*

*Office, seen from east.*

*Office, fountain added in 1956, doors to Cabaret-Theatre at far right.*

*East side detail of Office.*

◁ *South side detail of Office.*

*Office interior.*

*Office interior, west wall.*

*Office interior, east wall.*

*Drafting Room south side, Indian rock mounted on steps. (original petroglyph found on site.)*

*Drafting Room south side, left; annex-office en face; Guest Deck upper right. The annex-office was, in the original plan of Taliesin West, the dining room for the Fellowship. In 1952 FLLW moved the Fellowship dining room into the loggia on the other side of the building and converted this area into a small, private dining room. It has since been turned into an office for the drafting room clerical work.*

*Indian rock, annex-office and triangular pool.*

*Drafting Room and annex-office; Chinese Theatre mounted in desert masonry and contained within the wall.*

*Detail of pendants and Chinese Theatre, doors to annex-office beyond.*

*Elevation, section and details.*

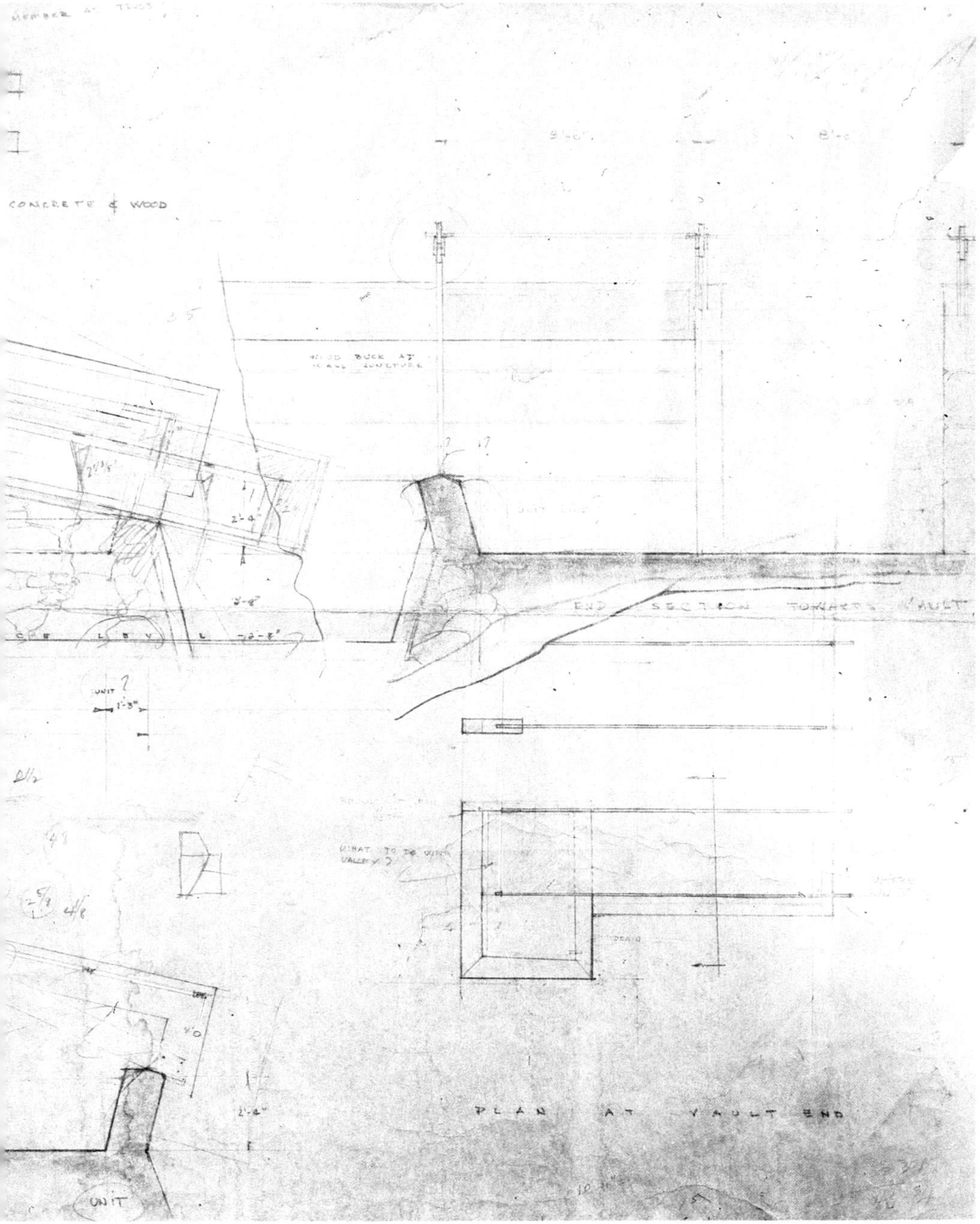

*Detail annex wall and roof, Drafting Room beyond. Hanging pendant at far right.*

*View toward annex-office.*

*Indian rock mounted on steps.*

*Drafting Room and Pergola, west end. Palm trees planted in 1959, subsequently removed when they began to tower over the building.*

◁ *Indian rock, Drafting Room beyond.*

*Detail of Drafting Room redwood trusses.*

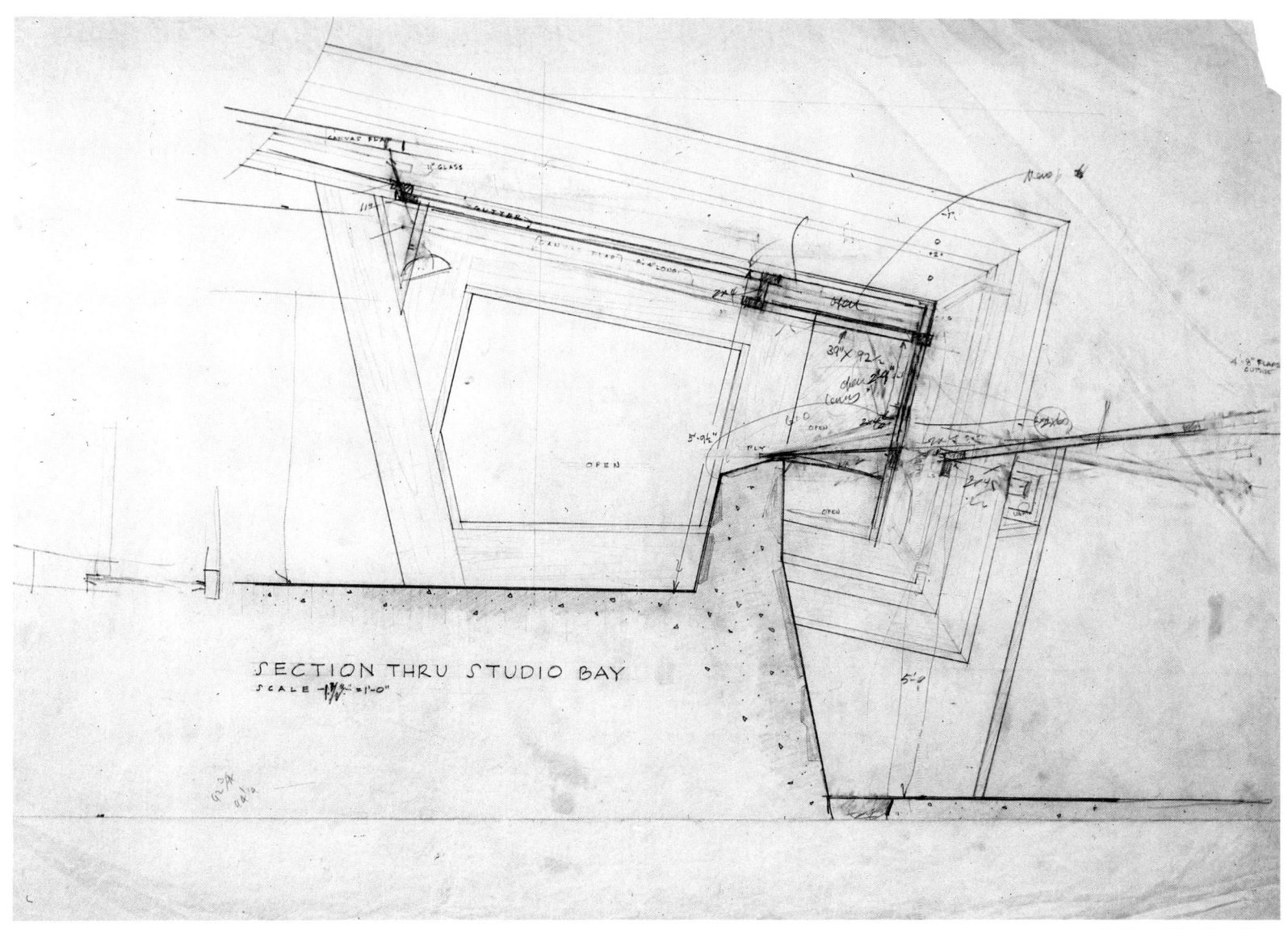

*Section of Drafting Room.*

◁ *Corner detail of Drafting Room.*

*Terrace between Office and Drafting Room, seen from doorway of the Cabaret-Theatre.*

Terrace

*View toward Drafting Room.*

*Pergola, along the north side of the Drafting Room.* ▷

*Pergola, looking west.*

*Drafting Room interior.*

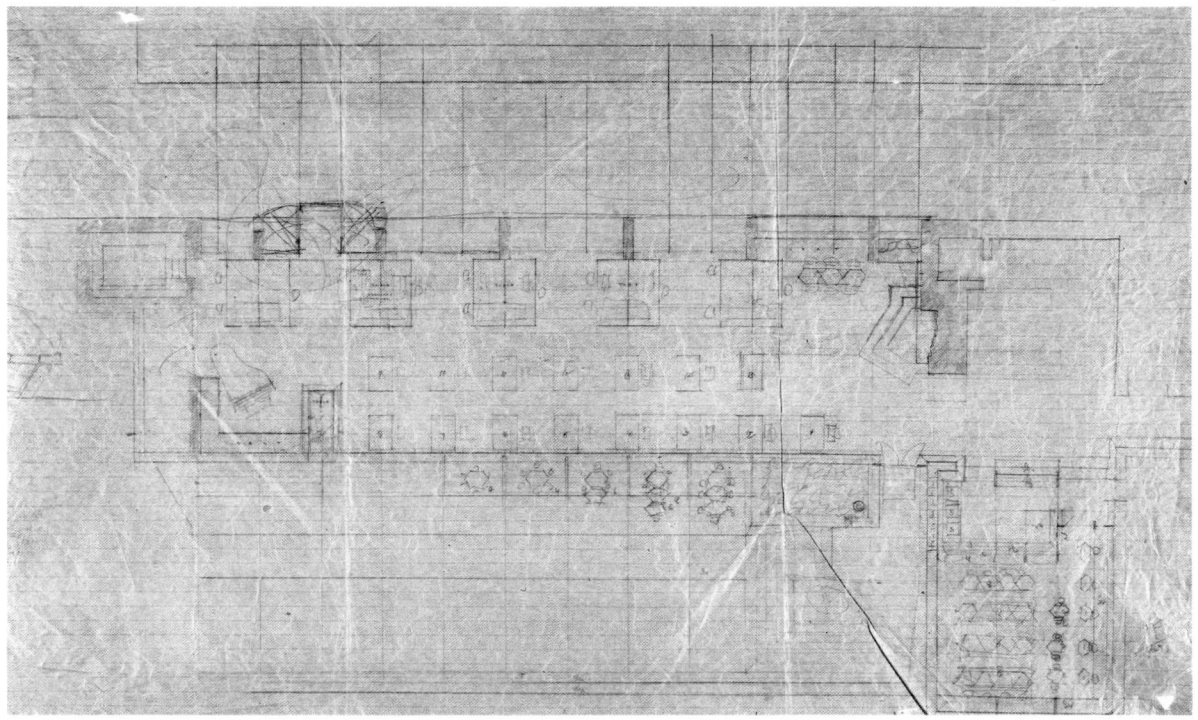

◁ *Drafting Room. interior, canvas replaced with plastic.*

*Plan of Drafting Room.*

◁ Upper part of Pergola.

Detail of Pergola and north side of Drafting Room.

*Water Tower and bridge from Guest Deck to roof terrace.*

*Guest Deck windows on right, Water Tower in center, roof terrace of original theatre on left. The new Cabaret-Theatre was started in 1949, this one turned into a gallery-conference room.*

*Water Tower.*

*Seen from Guest Deck north.*

*From Pergola looking east toward Water Tower.*

*Original theatre (1938) at close right, Dining Room glass windows center. Bell Tower beyond.*

*Kitchen wall mass to the right, Guest Deck on left, steps and Bell Tower center.*

*Bell Tower rising above kitchen wall mass; another Chinese Theatre mounted in desert masonry at steps to Guest Deck above.*

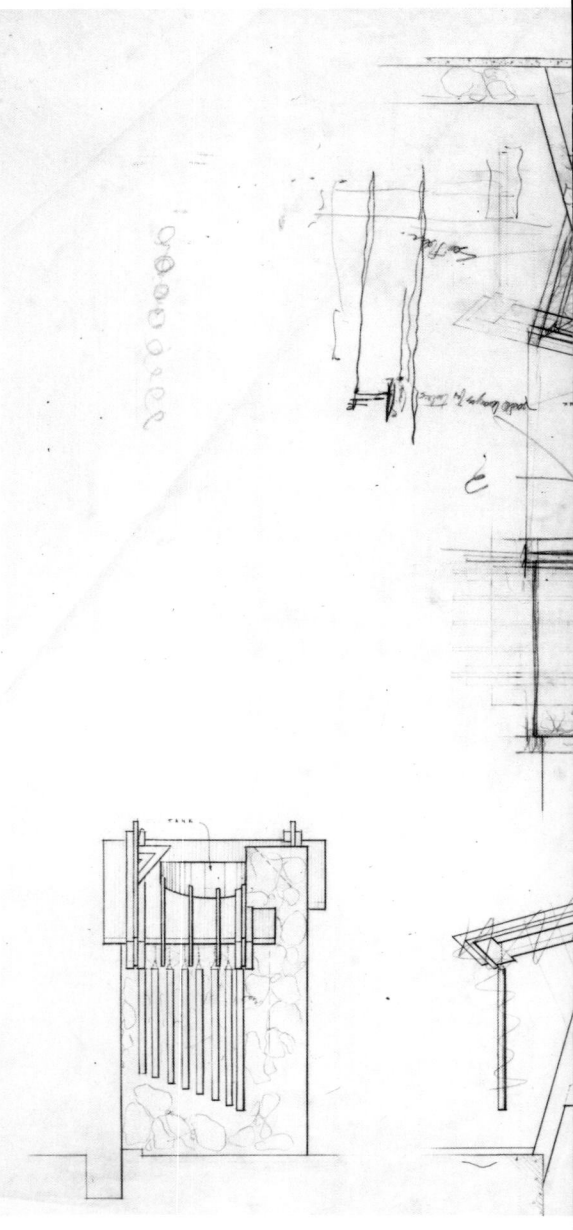

*View toward Bell Tower from the pool under the bridge.*

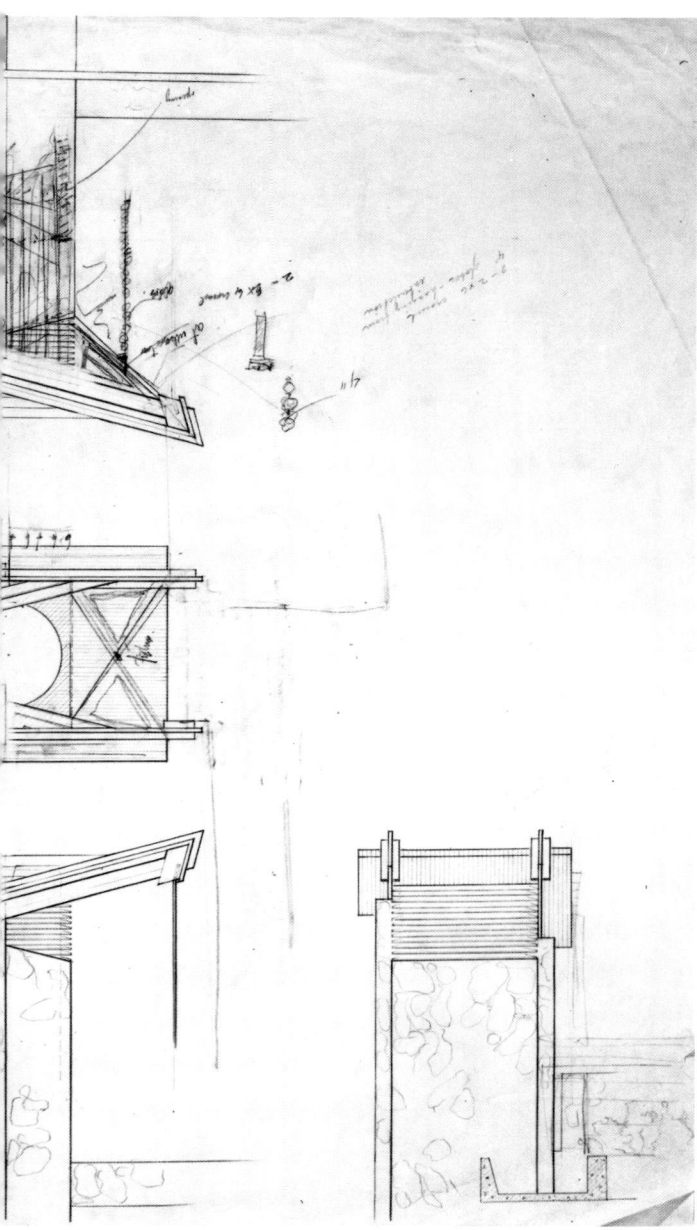

*Plan and elevations of Water Tower.*

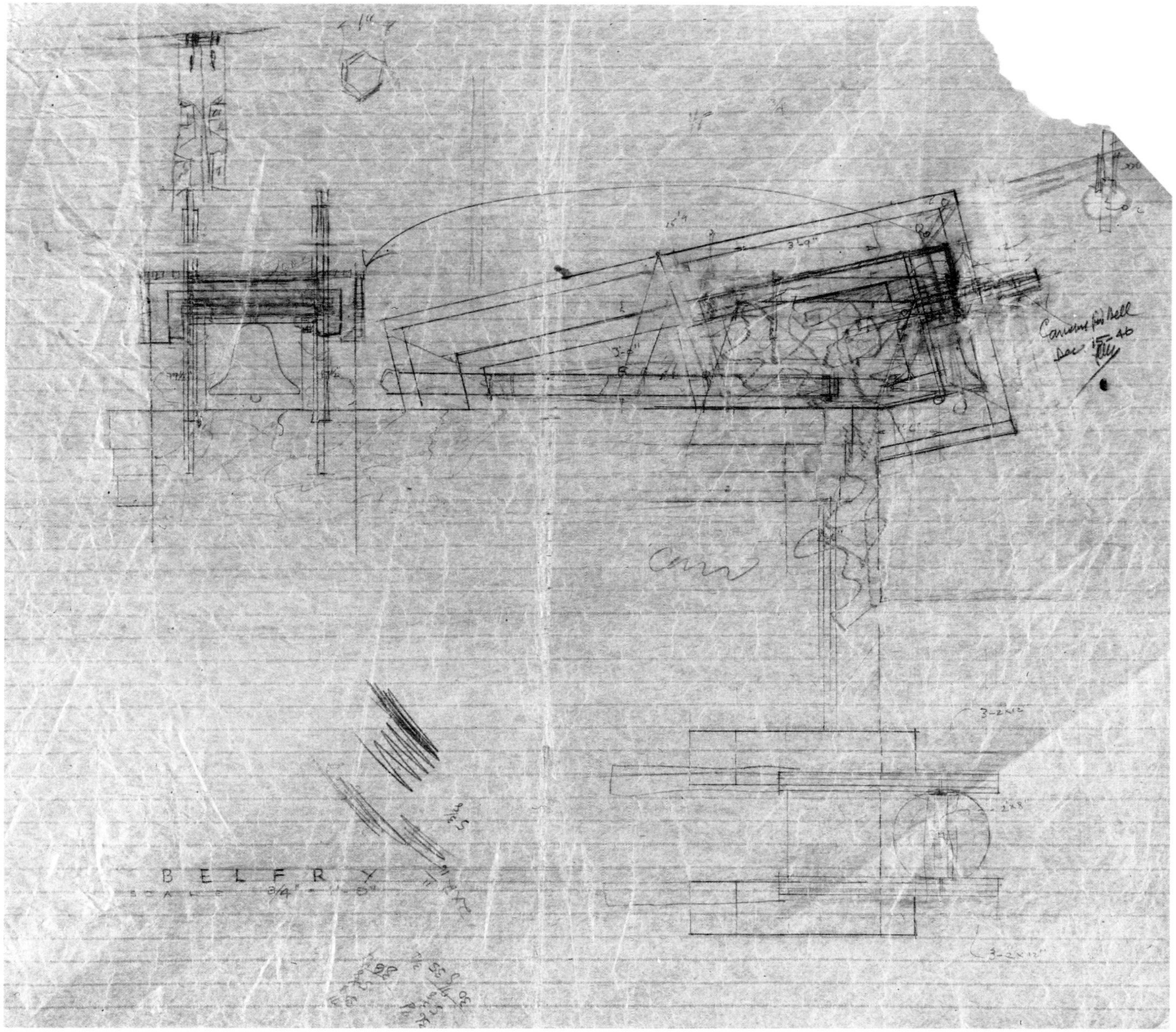

*Plan and elevations of Bell Tower.*

*Detail of masonry wall containing drawing vault at west end of Drafting Room. This was the first desert rubble-stone wall at Taliesin West, the "prototype" for all that followed.*

*Original theatre.*

*From Guest Deck out to Paradise Valley to the south.*

*Guest Deck, looking east.*

◁ *Looking from Guest Deck north to the citrus orchard (planned by the architect in early 1959, planted the morning he died on April, 1959). McDowell Mountains beyond.*

*Palo verde in bloom.*

*Breezeway, looking south (Dining Room on right, Main House on left).*

*Dining Room, first converted from open loggia to enclosed room in 1952, glass wall extended further in 1958.*

*Dining Room.*

*Dining Room with furniture based on design for Midway Gardens, made at Taliesin West in 1961.* ▷

*Sunset Terrace, steps leading to the Breezeway, Guest Deck above. Sunlight on the dentils of deck edge cast shadows on the steps below, typical of what the architect meant when he spoke of the "dotted-line" and "eye-music."*

◁ Chinese Theatre mounted in desert masonry, to the left of main entry to Garden Room.

Garden Room seen from gravel terrace.

Garden Room, from Sunset Terrace.

Garden Room, from bedroom wing. ▷

*Eastern facade of Garden Room.*

*Bedroom wing.*

Bougainvillea.

*Small court at north end of Garden Room, Dining Cove to the right.*

*Garden Room, north end; matching Sung vase on the shelf by the glass wall.*

◁ *Looking into small court from Dining Cove.*

*One of two Sung vases on the shelf; the glass window cut to allow the vase to slightly protrude outside.*

*Entrance to the Garden Room, door from the Sunset Terrace on the left.*

*Entrance to the Garden Room leading toward the stone "trough" for planting.*

*Looking toward entry.*

◁ *Looking toward Dining Cove, small court to the right.*

*Detail of ceiling.*

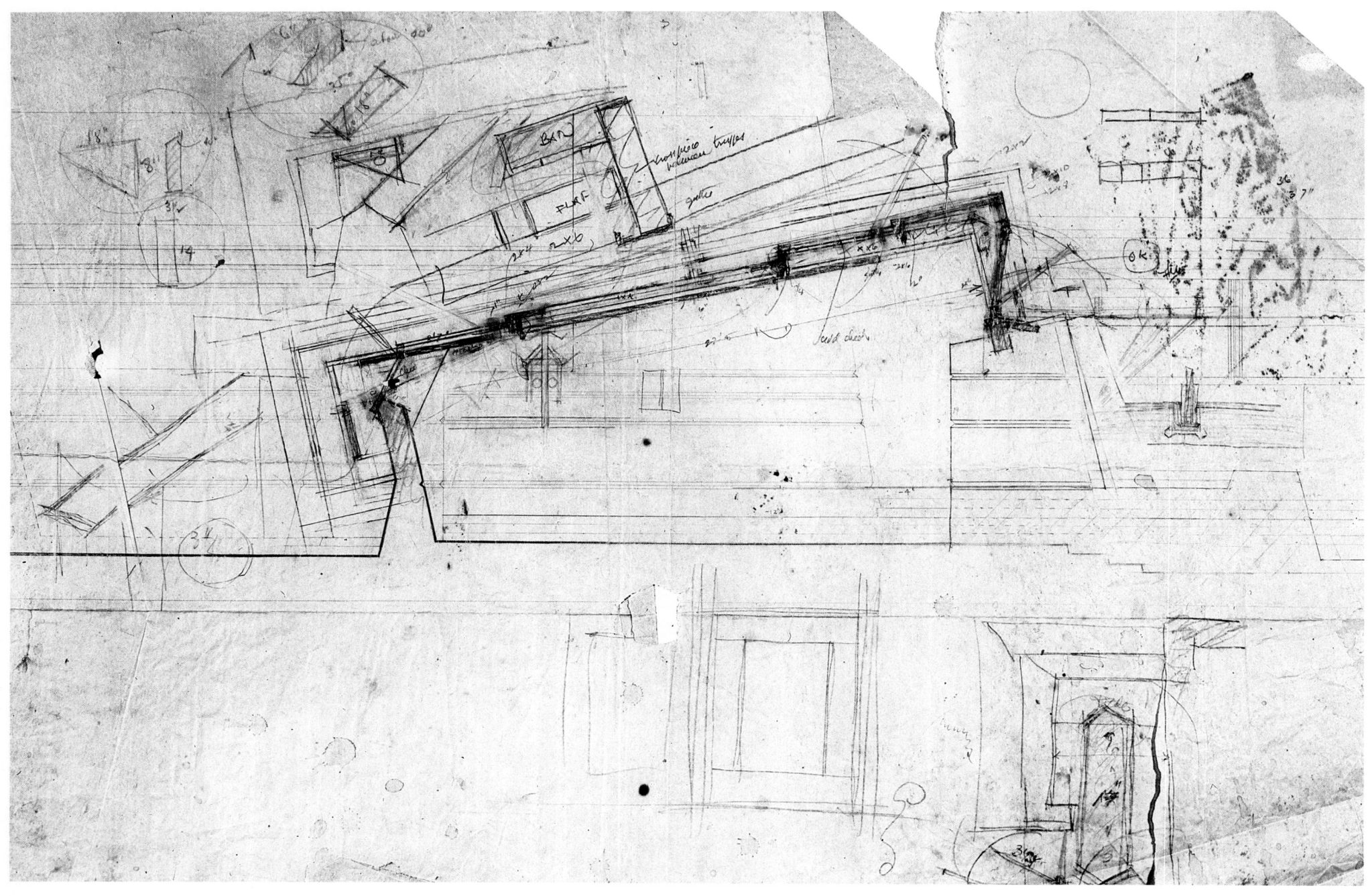

*Section of Garden Room.*

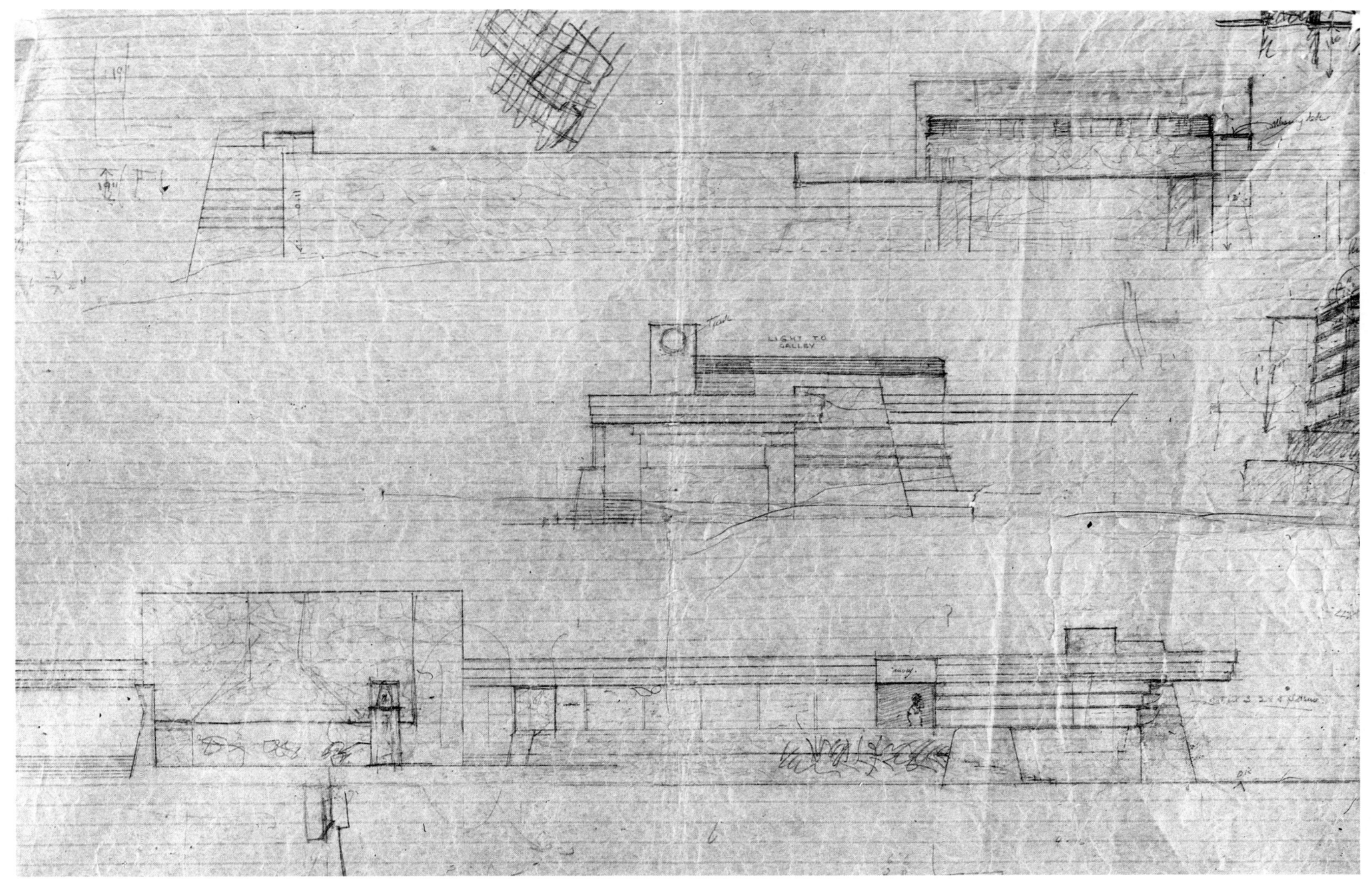

*Elevations of bedroom wing.*

◁ Garden Room, looking south from Dining Cove.

Garden Room.

*Garden Room, looking north.*

◁ *Garden Room, looking southwest toward Sunset Terrace.*

*Garden Room.*

*Garden Room, looking south.*

*Garden Room, with clerestory window, looking northeast toward mountain.*

*South end corner of Garden Room. Wood folding screen by Allen Lape Davison was a Christmas present to Frank Lloyd Wright in 1955. The screen is actually the plan of Taliesin West.*

*Glass works along garden window of bedroom wing.*

*Garden Room, detail of fireplace. Added in 1957, FLLW handpicked the stones for this mass and directed the placing of each one of them. The wooden forms were cut so that certain round boulders, covered with lichen, could protrude from the wall surface.*

*Music Pavilion roof rising beyond and above Cabaret Theatre*

*Music Pavilion, built in 1957 for the dance-drama productions created by the architect's daughter Iovanna Lloyd Wright. Sculpture by Heloise Crista.*

*Entrance to the Music Pavilion. Sculpture by Heroise Crista.*

*Music Pavilion, interior view from stage to house.*

*Music Pavilion, looking onto stage. Curtain bars swing back and fabric is rolled up, revealing further stage area beyond. All stage lighting hung directly from roof trusses as needed.*

*View from entrance of Cabaret-Theatre.*

*Cabaret-Theatre, interior. Tables open for dining, small serving kitchen located up the ramp behind the screen.*

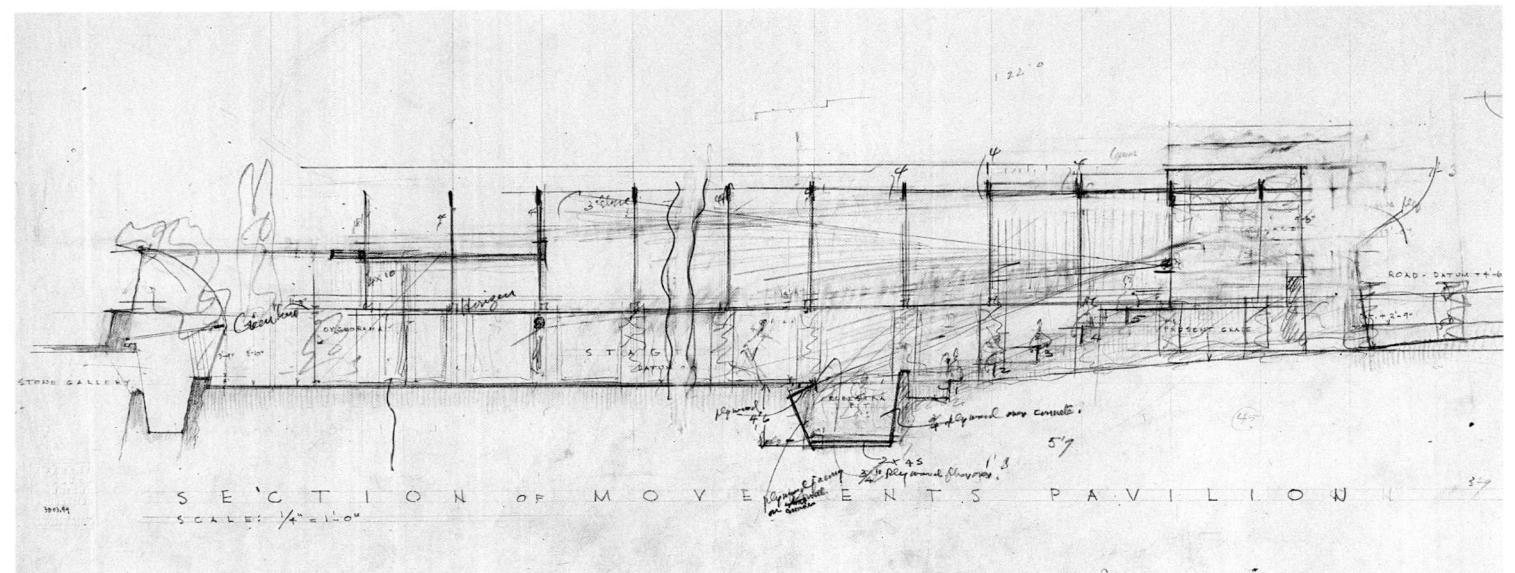

*Longitudinal section of Music Pavilion.*

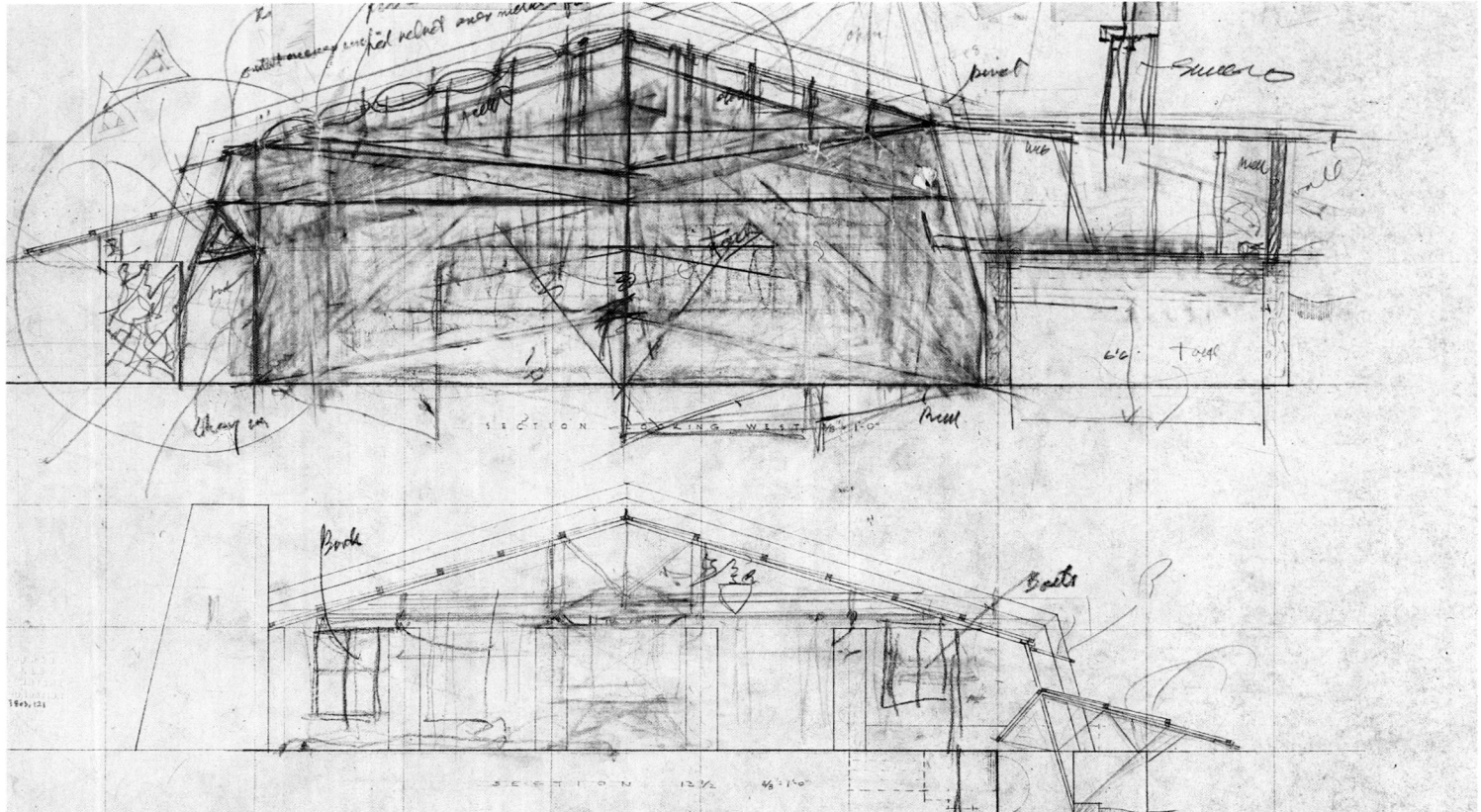

*Cross sections of Music Pavilion.*

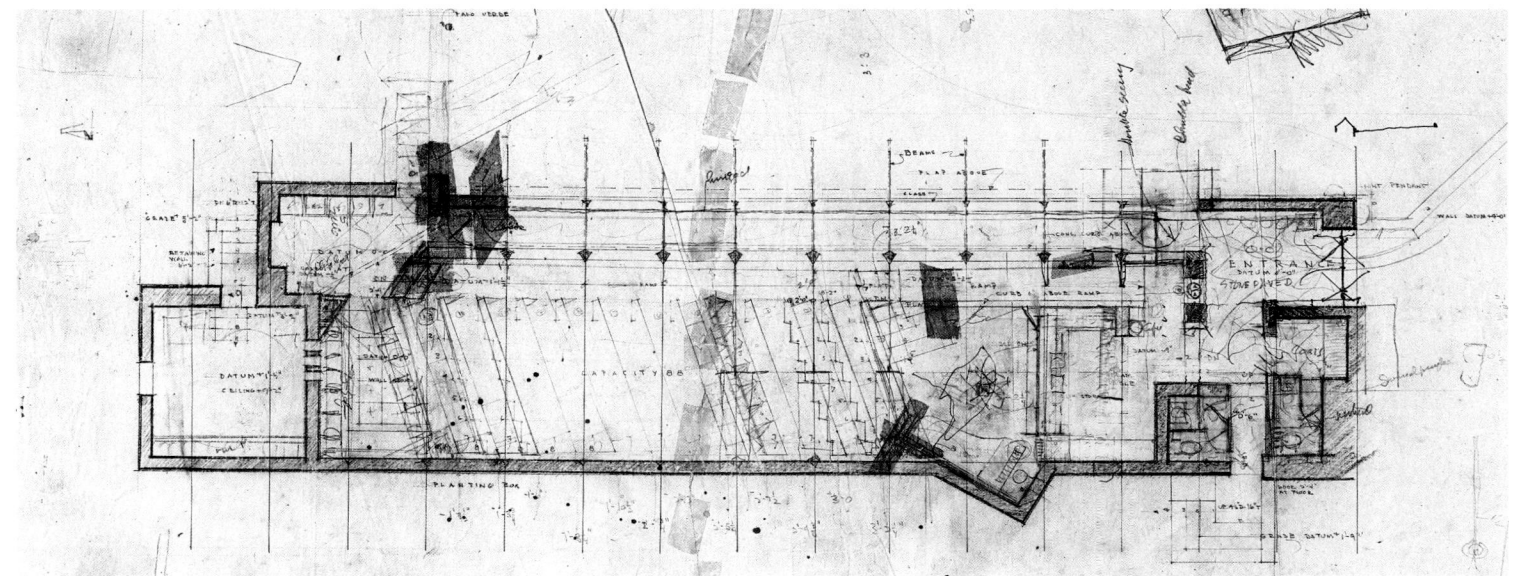
*Plan of Cabaret-Theatre.*

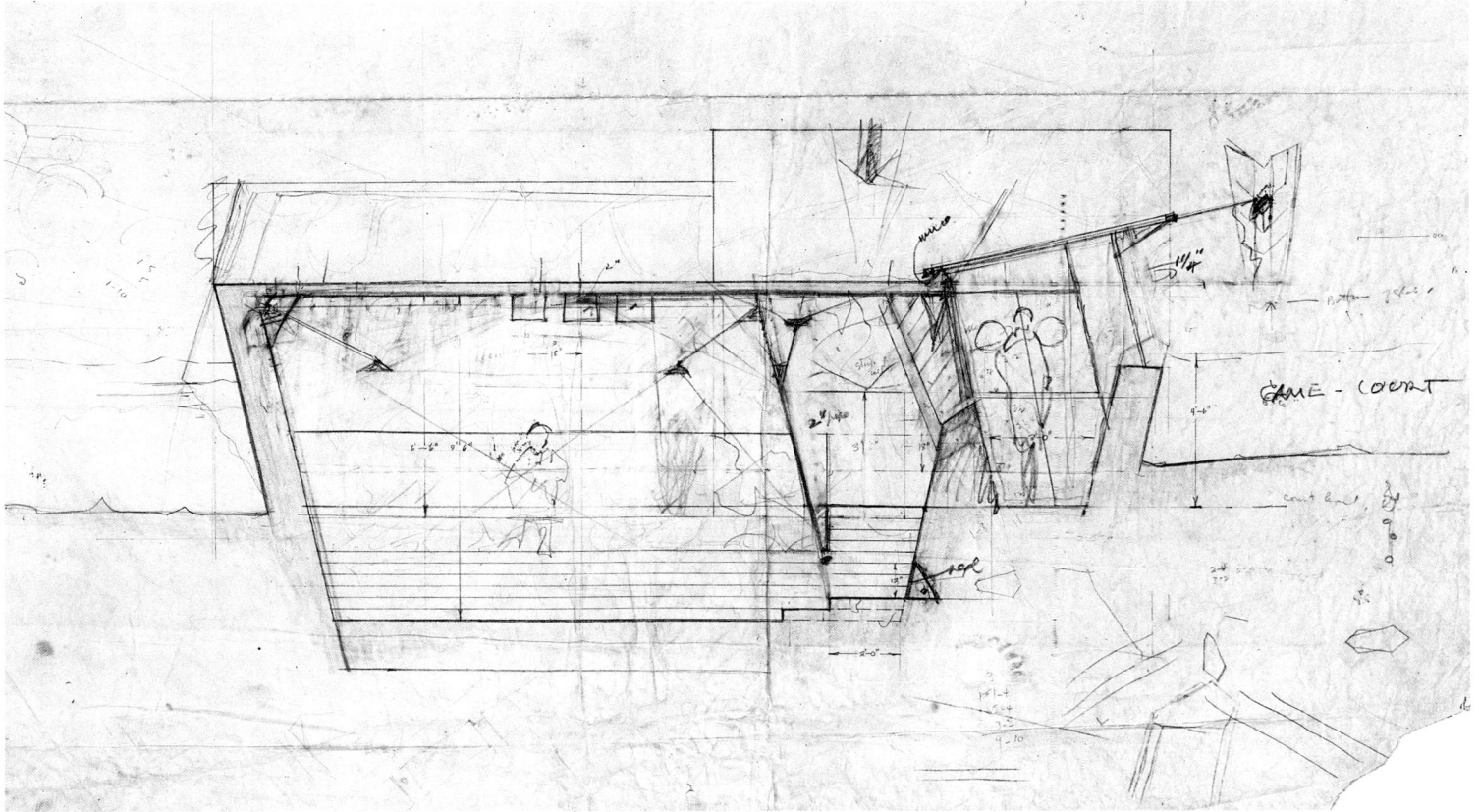
*Section of Cabaret-Theatre.*

*Taliesin in the desert.*

フランク・ロイド・ライトの住宅　第3巻
〈タリアセン・ウェスト〉

1989年11月7日初版発行
1992年1月10日再版発行

|企画・撮影|二川幸夫|
|文|ブルース・ブルックス・ファイファー|
|翻訳|玉井一匡|
|デザイン|細谷巖|
|発行者|二川幸夫|
|印刷・製本|日本写真印刷株式会社|
|発行|A.D.A. EDITA Tokyo Co., Ltd.|

東京都渋谷区千駄ヶ谷3-12-14
TEL.(03) 3403-1581(代)

禁無断転載

ISBN4-87140-545-1 C1352